Going In To Find Out

A Spiritual Discovery of Self

Insights of Babaji

Heather Cronrath

First Printing

International Standard Book Number: 978-1-58776-917-7

Printed In The United States Of America

Cover design By NetPublications Inc.

Cover photo by Heather Cronrath

Author's photo by itsuphoto.com

675 Dutchess Turnpike, Poughkeepsie, NY 12603
www.hudsonhousepub.com (800) 724-1100

PREFACE

In 2005 an interesting phenomenon occurred. I had been meditating, with and without a lot of success for about 5 years. Over time I had begun to hear messages during my meditations, but there was no consistency to them or reliability. Then suddenly, the tenor of them began to change and I thought I should attempt to sit at my computer while meditating in the hopes of capturing some of the messages. The more I did this, the more they began to change until they took on the format you will find in this book as well as the first book.

As the meditations became more focused, I also heard "book, book, book" which I chose to ignore for the first four months. My reward for that was having these meditations stop in August 2005. I was directed to read and study more and was especially directed to Yogananda's "The Second Coming of Christ, Awakening the Christ Within." The two volume set had just been released by the Self Realization Fellowship and was the culmination of over 50 years work compiling Yoganada's meditations on the New Testament. I promptly bought a copy and spent the next three months reading and meditating on this material. Having completed my task, I naively thought the meditations would resume, but was again instructed – "Book, Book, Book." So I quickly assembled the meditations in a loose leaf format and published "We Are All In This Alone – A Journey to Self – Insights of Babaji" in December 2005. The meditations began again in January 2006.

This is a compilation of those meditations. While they appear to be similar to the original meditations, there is a different energy to them. When they were being shared with me, the strength, love and intention of the words was much stronger and clearer. During the process of editing and formatting this book these same feelings have been very present as well.

For those of you who may not have experienced the first book, I would like to share a bit about Babaji. He is known as the Yogi Christ and is the first Yogi in the line that completed with Yogananda. He is believed to still be alive somewhere in the Himalayas. For me it has been a life long acquaintance with him, even before I knew anything about him.

As a child I heard voices, which I thought was normal, until about the age of five at which point I made a "conscious" decision to turn off the voices. While I might have made that decision in my head, I now know that the voices never stopped, I just stopped listening. In hindsight I can say that I was always aware of a voice with a different quality in my head, but I paid it no heed. In my early twenties I was told by a psychic that I had once heard voices and that I no longer listened. I was informed that this was not appreciated. While I thought it an odd thing to say to someone, it did begin to rattle around in my head and the memories of life up to the age of five returned slowly. It was a long process back to hearing the voices, but the night during a meditation class when I was asked to deliver a message I was informed that the message was from Babaji. As I laid there communicating within my own mind, the quality of the "voice" was very familiar. I asked, "Were you the voice I used to hear as a child?" and the reply was "We are the voice you have always heard, but you chose not to listen."

I realize that for many this story may seem a bit far fetched or unbelievable and from time to time it has seemed that way to me, but I can tell you that I have come to realize that I have been truly blessed with the information and messages that are given to me. I share them with all of you in both of these books, just as Babaji requested.

A quick word about the title, "Going In To Find Out." This title "came to me" one day and seemed to stick. I credited myself with being rather clever, but as with many things in my life, I now realize that it was Babaji who gave me the title. As you experience the meditations and lessons within these pages, you too will realize that the only way to find out is to go in.

Many of the spellings found within these pages are more British than American English. This is how they were given to me during the meditations and therefore, have been left as dictated. The cadence of the language is also Babaji's not mine. So enjoy the flow and the poetry of the writing.

Thank you for your support. I know that this book will be a lovely guide along the path to enlightenment. Remember that the Soul's journey is often not known by you consciously, but the Soul knows how to get where it needs to go.

Enjoy the journey and remember to laugh.

Namaste

Heather Cronrath
August 2010

FORWARD

This book is not meant to be read straight through, although you can give it a try. It is designed, rather, to be opened at random. The purpose for this is that it allows you to remove your own prejudices and receive the message or messages that would most help you in that moment to move along the path to peace, joy, enlightenment and insight.

You may receive a different meditation each time you open the book. Other times you will open to the same or very similar meditations. I would advise that when this occurs, it is a great time to get the lesson and work on the information presented. My first book was originally published as a spiral bound. One of the early users of the book believed that she was constantly receiving the same meditation because the book's binding had some kind of memory where it opened. To rid herself of this annoying aspect, she purchased a trade paperback version. The first time she opened the book, it took her to the exact same meditation. As she said to me later, "Guess it is time to start working on that rather than just reading it each time."

So, allow the book and Babaji to help you find the right place to be at any time. I use this practice myself and have been forced to admit a number of times, especially when experiencing challenging life moments, that taking a page from my own book usually solves the problem.

This book is a huge gift, not only to me, but for each of us. It is a lovely roadmap to guide all of us through the shoals of life and to do so with love, insight and most of all humour. If you can't laugh at most of life, it becomes a rather long journey.

Enjoy your journey.

Heather Cronrath

This book is dedicated to all those that are willing to battle their fears, demons, dragons and "I don't want to," to find their Self. The journey is often lonely, twisting and scary, but the reward of freedom, joy and fully knowing YOU is worth the effort. I want to thank my clients, friends and family for their constant encouragement, feedback and support. Finally, there is always Babaji to thank for his wisdom, knowledge and on-going patience as we wend our way towards Self.

Take a deep breath and start the ride.

Heather Cronrath

PREPAREDNESS - READINESS

Are you ready to live your life?

Are you ready to be alive or are you just sitting in the chair of life waiting for something to happen?

Life is about action, about movement, about forward movement/propulsion. It is about looking at your situation and making life affirming decisions about the direction your life is to take. Most of you sit and wait. You may be very busy in this sitting and waiting mode, but that is really what you are doing. You are letting life happen to you. What do you want to happen? What do you want to do with your life? What do you want to be? Some of you may say that you are too old and life has passed you by. You might be 20 or 25 or 40 or 50 or older. We tell you that if you are reading this and you are breathing than you are still alive. Some of you will say you are sick or fat or tired or unable to "do" anything. Some will say they don't have the education or the skills for what they want to do. We say that all things are possible if you get into action.

So, you are too tired or too fat or ill. Begin to move. Move at whatever pace **you** can move. At first it may be a slow walk and maybe that walk is just around the entire inside of your house twice a day, but we promise you that you can move in some way. If you are wheelchair bound you can move in your chair. If you suffer from paralysis move in your mind. Begin to visualize your Self the way that athletes do. See your Self walking around the house or just the room. If walking is hard for you walk slowly, but begin to visualize your Self jogging a bit or walking faster. Take wherever you are right now and just do something because it will be your fist step to freedom from the belief that you "can not" and we want you to leave this behind.

If you don't have the skills you need for something begin to acquire them. Go to school if you can or begin to read about your topic. Find someone that does what you wish you were doing and talk to them. Try to find a job in the area that interests you. It may not be the job you "wish" for but if it begins to expose you to that which you desire you will have begun the journey.

You are all very Self-defeating. If it is not presented to you, if you have to be in action to get it, if you feel time has passed you by, you give up your dreams. Stop telling your Self the stories of CAN'T and begin to live your life in CAN. Possibilities abound that are unseen but they are waiting for you so begin the journey forward to life.

We leave in love and wish you happiness year-round.
Namaste

PAIN

How much pain are you in? It could be physical pain; it could be mental or emotional. Most pain is a combination of physical and mental/emotional for the feelings of pain manifest most readily in the body. You could be experiencing pain from physical ailments. Your joints could be aching or sore, you could suffer from greater maladies that cause you a constant flow of pain. In some cases it is difficult to distance your Self from the physical pain for it seems so pervasive. Pain is a reality, but what you choose to do with it is a choice. You can have pain and choose not to suffer. You can have pain and choose to put your mind somewhere else. Or you can choose to acknowledge your pain and seek to find relief from it. I hear *"How?"* for some of you despair that you cannot distance your Self from pain, but we shall explore this phenomenon.

Let us work with the mind first. What happens when you think sad thoughts? Do you feel uplifted, enlivened, or happy? You often use the terms "broken heart" or "it felt like a knife in my stomach." Most of the time you are referring to some mental experience that you are manifesting through words to be in your body. No other person can inflict pain upon you without your permission. That is a fact. It may sound harsh to some for there are many humans that are masterful at inflicting emotional upheaval, but again we state they cannot affect you if you do not allow it to be so. You can choose whether to listen to others opinions of you or not. If you do not hold your Self in high esteem then it is easy for others to inflict mental pain for you willingly allow it and some might say attract it.

Why do you want this pain? Let us take a situation of an ended relationship. Now this relationship could have ended through attrition or death. Either way, the person is no longer in your life. What are your emotions - sadness, anger, grief, loss? You can choose to experience these and that is a big part of the human condition, but how long you continue to grieve the end of the relationship is completely within your control. The past is the past and you can dwell in it as long as you choose, but whilst you are dwelling there life continues to happen right before your eyes. So what do you choose – pain of loss or life with possibilities?

Now if you have physical pain what can you do for it or about it? If you have a disease can you manage the illness enough to put the pain aside? If it is aches and pains from aging or too much weight or not enough weight, can you alter your behaviours to be more honoring of your body; this vessel that moves you from place to place? If you cannot find a solution of setting aside the pain, can you work with the mental aspects of your Self to choose not to suffer from the pain? It is possible and again it is completely within your control No one can tell you the level of pain you can tolerate, but you would be surprised how you can ignore pain when something joyful or uplifting comes along. Think about how willing you are to push through pain if you know that you are going to a party, or seeing someone you have not seen in a long time or whatever the happy event could be. This tells us that if you can find joy, happiness and love in the things that surround you, you can triumph over the pain in ways you never thought possible. Many of the medicines that are given to you for pain control change the chemistry of the brain so that you don't pay attention to the pain. Why not try to change the chemistry of your brain with joy, laughter, connection and love? Those are the best drugs there are in the universe.

We leave you in joy.
Namaste

FEAR

Fear is pervasive; it colors most of what the human condition feels and looks like. You live in a fear based society filled with terrors seen and unseen. What is there to fear?

Death?
Pain?
Destruction?
Loss?
Germs?

Take a moment and think about something you recently feared. Now we are not asking you to think of something horrendous unless that is what has just occurred. We are asking you to think of the last time you felt fear or even anxiety for that is like "mini-fear." What made you anxious? Was it the fear that was making you upset within your control? By this we mean did you have the ability to stop the action or thought? Was the thing you feared worth that amount of stress on your body? What was the outcome? Did something bad happen or did it just dissipate? How much of the anxiety and fear were simply based in your mind or belief system? Did your fear change the outcome?

If you begin to practice walking calmly forward in life pushing aside all the fears and concerns about, *"what if and maybe's,"* you will find much greater energy and strength for dealing with the realities of life. Most of you live in *"might be's"* and *"could happen's"* rather than simply allowing life to unfold. If you allow life to happen and you remain calm, it is amazing what you can deal with in a calm, centered way.

Now look at another fear. First ask, is it real? Don't begin to give your Self evidence of how it might occur, the question really is -"Is it occurring right now?" If the fear is motivated by something in your head that is trying to upset and derail you, stop for a moment and re-center. Is the fear REAL? Does it have any basis in fact or is it something you make-up to keep you from living your life fully? If you begin to dissect the fear or anxious feeling bit by bit, it becomes less of a monster and more of a puzzle to solve. Be real and honest with your Self and you will begin to see the fears lessen and disappear and reality take you into the next life phase.

We leave you with loving fearlessness.
Namaste

CONNECTION

How do you connect with other human beings?

Do you offer your Self to humanity to experience you fully?

Do you withhold your Self so that others don't truly know you?

Do you this from a place of fear, privacy or distrust?

Do you have several "personalities" available for people so that you can choose which one of you to allow out at that moment?

Just take a few moments to think about who you are in the world.

Now some of you are very withholding about your life and your life experiences. You allow your Self to be caught up in society's conventions of right and wrong. You allow your lives to be driven by judgment – yours and others - and it keeps you from living fully. Perhaps you have something about you or your past that you judge to be less than elegant or less than acceptable to society at large. To whom is it really unacceptable? Does society really care or do you care or have you been taught you should care?

Sometimes it helps other humans to connect if you have the bravery to be who you are for them. If you use your mistakes, foibles, hurts and life lessons to help others see that these things are only transitory you perform a true service in the world. These things do not last if you do not allow them to color the future. What we are saying is that your past should only be used as an example. However, if you allow your past to be what defines you, then your whole future is colored with these “mistakes” or missteps. What do you have to hide?

When you hide things from others you keep a part of you locked away from humanity. This is not to say that everyone you meet needs to know all about you, but what we are saying is that if you keep these things hidden then you cannot fully express who you are and for what you stand. Embrace your life experiences as just that, life experiences. Then use the experiences to make a brighter future not only for you but for others you encounter. If you see someone struggling with something you have survived or triumphed over, how does it hurt you to put out a hand of compassion to say, “I have been there too and walked through it to the other side.” If you share these moments with others you give hope and you give comfort and you share humanity.

Try to spend the next week connecting with others. Do not strain, but simply notice where you begin to withhold or retreat. Notice others who might be confused or in pain and see if you can connect with them in a way that helps them through this time.

We leave you in connection.
Namaste

OBEDIANCE

How will are you to give up your wants to have what you need? There is a lot of unrest amongst you all when it comes to the things you "want." Take a few moments to make a list of your wants. What do you want? Again, we ask that you be completely honest and not make a list of things you think others would approve of, but rather the things that come floating to your mind when we say "wants."

Now, look at the list and evaluate the nature of your desires. Are they material in nature or are they about interaction and relationship? Perhaps you might want to categorize the list into types of "wants" to get a better idea of your desires. As you read this list, what emotions or thoughts begin to occur? Do you allow your Self to float into the world of wanting? Do you begin to give your Self a long list of why you can't have or shouldn't have your wants? Do you stop your Self because getting what you want is too hard or would take too long or seems impossible? Sit with the list for a day or so. Edit the list, rearrange the list, evaluate the list, add or subtract from the list. Get acquainted with your wants and desires.

When you have spent this time playing with your list we would like you to make a new list. This one should be what you need. Now this is not limited to your basic needs for survival such as food, shelter, clothing, but rather what do you truly NEED to be happy, to be joyful? What must you have in order for your life to work in the way you imagine or dream? In order for you to begin to address your list of wants there must be something that you need or some things that you need. What about you keeps you from having what you claim to want? How centered are you in knowing who you are and where you are going? How content are you within your Self that you can be at peace with your Self where you are right now? Compare your list of needs with your want list. See how they interact; notice how they have nothing in common. Then take a moment to realize that you are more focused on one list than the other. Which list seems more important? Which list is the "gotta haves" and which challenges you more? "Needs" take work because they are at the core of your being. If you need more Spirituality, then you must dedicate your Self to that task. If you need more connection with others, it requires that you reach out and make an effort to share your Self. If you need better health it requires you change your habits of eating and exercise. Which brings us back to our original question –

"How willing are you to be obedient to your needs?"

Please work on these in love and compassion.

We leave you in love.
Namaste

PAIN

How painful does it have to be to make you stop? How often during your day do you experience pain? Now the pain can be either mental or physical or it could be both. What is causing the pain? Are you not moving your body enough or is it too much? Do you feed your Self foods that cause you to ache or feel less than perfect? Are you not eating enough or drinking enough water? Do you live in your subconscious mind and worry or fret or plan or over-think . Have you just ended a relationship with a person or a job? Are you out of sorts with your family, friends or place of work? Maybe you don't think of it as actual pain, but think about how your thoughts cause you to feel stress, unrest, upset or distraction.

How willing are you to stop the pain? Is the pain so familiar to you that it seems "normal?" Do you not even notice the pain? Is the pain within your control? It would be surprising to you how much of your discomfort and upset is within your control for you have the power to change the behaviours that contribute to the pain in most cases. We are not talking about catastrophic illness or surgeries that perhaps have caused the on-set of pain, but rather the day-to-day living that produces ill health or mental upset.

Think about what hurts. If it is physical do you know the causes? Are there things that you could do to stop the pain? Could you begin to move your body more to begin to make it more limber again? Could you stop eating certain foods that might be contributing to the pain? Do you know if you are allergic to anything whether it be food or plants or molds? There are many causes for physical pain that are not commonly known yet are reasonably simple to fix. Perhaps you are exercising too much or not eating correctly because you are concerned about your body image. Is your diet appropriate to live a pain free life? Do you consume too much alcohol or sugar or do you smoke? Do you maintain your oral hygiene? Take an assessment of your vessel called a body and take note of where you might be in need of repair or overhaul. Again we say that this does not have to be a huge expense or problem, but rather it is a task of bringing your awareness to the problem so that you can put appropriate action in place to create peace.

Now to the pain caused by your mind. How often do you create upset, unhappiness, worry, fear, judgment in your own mind? Do you find your Self to be enough? Do you praise your Self for your accomplishments and deeds or do you beat your Self up because it is not enough? Do you think that other people are controlling your ability to be happy or make money or live fully? Do you fear the future or wish for more control over your destiny? Take stock of your thoughts. How many of your thoughts in a day are positive and uplifting about your Self? How many times in a day do you depreciate your Self either out loud or internally? If others spoke to you as you speak to your Self would it be a positive relationship?

Most pain control or management is within your control. Decide to set your Self free and you will be amazed at the energy and uplift you experience.

We leave in love.
Namaste

CONFUSION

What is right?
What is wrong?
What should you do?
What shouldn't you do?
Who should you love?
Where should you live?
How should you earn a living?
Are you making enough money?
Are you kind enough?
What should you eat?
Should you diet?
How should you exercise?

This is just a sampling of what goes through your minds every moment you are awake and much of the time you sleep. If you don't believe that, look at your dreams! The human condition is constantly questioning in some way how they get through the day. What would your day be like if you just were in silence with your Self, allowing for each moment to occur and not judging or questioning it? The sounds in your heads are deafening at times and they overwhelm you. You lead lives of great stress. Your technology allows for you never to be out of communication. You are now available 24/7 as you say. Between the computers, cell phones, faxes and global economy, you are little cities that never sleep. Because you have the technology you feel you must use it. How many of you can remember when the telephone was attached to the wall and you could only go as far as the cord allowed? Was your life more difficult then? Or was it just more simple? As these conveniences have come into your lives it has required that you become more "on call" than in the past and this allows for less time to contemplate and reflect upon your life.

When was the last time you just sat, with your Self in silence? No television, no phone of any kind, no computer, no DVD player - Just you and the silence. What does that seem like to you as you read it? Does it seem wonderful or scary or stupid or boring or dull? Think about your reaction. Why are you afraid to be alone with your Self? Do you find your Self to be a good friend? Are you interesting to be with or do you need some tool or other person to make you interesting or whole?

Let us return to the voices in your head that we described in the beginning. What do you talk to your Self about? Are your internal conversations uplifting and full of possibility and love? Or are your personal one-on-one chats with your Self about all the things that you have not done or should do or must do? Are they about your failures or your success? The first thing to do if you want to clear the confusion is to begin to re-dialogue your internal playback. Move to the positive, move to the uplifting and away from the judgment and pain. As you begin to lighten up on your Self you will begin to find that the stream of consciousness is less overwhelming and more enlightening. As this begins to occur you will find a better opportunity to live in the moment and not in the past with your mistakes or in the future with your fears.

We leave you in quiet contemplation of Self.
Namaste

WORTHINESS

Do you deserve a happy life?
Do you deserve ease and abundance and love?
Do you deserve friends, family and associates?
Do you deserve to be alive?

Now some of this may seem extreme and most of you would answer "Yes" to the questions, but we ask you to delve deeper into the meaning of those questions and into your own psyche. What do you deserve? This is not what you want or think you want or would like to have, for most of you can rattle that off easily, but we want to know what you think you deserve.

First sit with that word
DESERVE

What does it mean to you?
Is it something you must earn?
Is it something to which you are entitled?
What do you have to do in order to deserve?
Do you have to do anything?

So now ask your Self – Do I deserve a happy life? Allow all the answers to come up. Listen to the loud answer or answers and then listen to the more subtle and quiet answers. What are the small voices or protests that arise? These are your demons if you will. These are the voices, the thoughts that are keeping you from having this "happy" life. They reside within you not without. YOU are what keeps you have from having a happy life. It is that simple. It is those small voices in your head that judge and convict you. They are the "people" that are keeping you from moving away, taking a new job, marrying the person of your dreams, leaving the person that "controls" you or forcing you to stay in the same place in life. YOU are the one that determines your worthiness, your "deserve-ability" if you will.

So the next time you think you don't deserve something, spend some time with your Self to determine why YOU think that you cannot have the life you were meant to live.

We leave in great love and contemplation.
Namaste

JUDGMENT

Do you judge things as they occur?

Do you place right/wrong, good/bad, easy/hard, nice/mean upon things that occur and people you meet?

Are all things necessary to judge and rate?

Must all things be valued in this way?

Notice your Self as you go through a day. How often do you stop to analyze a situation whether out loud or silently in your head? Begin to notice how many times during the day you label or judge an event, a moment or an encounter. Then begin to observe how long your mind continues to go back to the event or conversation or encounter. How much time do you lose replaying the entire occurrence? Is it worth the time? A driver cuts you off in traffic. How many things do you allow to come out of your mouth or go through your head about the idiocy of that driver? How does it affect your mood? How does it affect your driving? Does it color the rest of the day or your next meeting? Does any of this constant replay change that person's ability to drive? Did the person do it consciously or unconsciously? Does it matter?

How much time do you spend listening to gossip or wanting to "be in the know" at work? Does most of this information impact your ability to do your job? Is it necessary information that you need to be a happy, informed and effective employee? Do you allow others upsets or opinions about other co-workers to color your opinion? If you do, what does that do to your productivity, your satisfaction with your job? Does most of it matter?

You spend an awful lot of time watching the “game tapes” of your life. The “plays” have been made, the scores have been posted and you all want to go back and replay the game or rehash what you “could have done” or “should have done” or “might have done” or “wished you had done.” Does anything change from all of that? Perhaps you will be smarter or quicker or less affected the next time, but mostly what occurs is an incredible loss of productivity, creativity, happiness and time.

Please take the time to catalogue and watch/observe your thoughts about the judgments of your daily living. You may be surprised how very little you live in the moment and how much of your life is lived in the past and in the future. Live now and live in joy

We leave in love.
Namaste

WALLS

How many walls do you build in your life?

How do you keep people out or thoughts out or activities out?

Do you wall your Self off from others with reasons that are conscious or do you just find your Self living behind a wall?

Do they make you feel safe?

Are they put there to keep you away or others?

Stop and think for a moment. What is your biggest wall? How long has it been there? Why do you want to live behind a barrier to communication? Do you put up small walls or temporary walls during the day? If they are temporary, how long do they remain? Are there signs that they were still there after you believed you have taken them down? Do you use walls to punish? Exclude? Hurt?

Many walls are put in place as a form of Self-survival and preservation. There is something in the human condition that thinks that the smaller the space the safer you are. Is this true? In a smaller space there is less chance to escape. There is less comfort as you cannot put in larger more comfortable furniture. You can not relax as easily in small spaces as large. If you do not believe us, simply go sit in your closet for a day. We will tell you that after a few minutes you will begin to feel very uncomfortable and confined, yet you do this to your Self psychically all the time.

You wall your Self off thinking you can control the hurt or flow of information, but we are here to tell you that all you do is begin to entomb your Self in a place without support, society or friends. It is lonely behind the walls. Look at your new housing developments. Are they open so that you can meet your neighbors and interact or are they walled off villas, some even with powered gates to keep you "safe" and apart from the rest of humanity? Do not live in a gated community within your Soul. Throw open the walls and move out into the world and begin to communicate and interact and love your fellow man and you will find connections and opportunities and joy that is at this time unknown to you.

We leave in freedom and expansion.
Namaste

CONFUSION

What is right?
What is wrong?
How should you be in life?
How do you allow the turmoil of your mind to keep you stuck?

Take a few days to listen to your Self. Take notes if you have the time. What are the thoughts, judgments, condemnations, upheavals, upsets and accusations that you rain upon your Self in each day, each hour and in each moment? Do you ever stop roiling the waters of your psyche and just sit in stillness and peace? We have suggested that you meditate at least five minutes each day and are hopeful that you could find at least two minutes in the five that allow for silence. Five would be magnificent. The silence is at the core or center of your being. So if you are feeling "off center" perhaps it is because you do not travel to the center of your being to rest. This is where bliss resides, peace, contentment and enlightenment. The best information you will receive will come to you in the silence, not the constant chatter and upheaval you think is living.

You live in an information age and think that more input is better, but we would disagree. Remember the phrase "Silence is golden?" There is a reason for this statement. The void is the place for true healing, for true enlightenment and for true peace. A void contains nothing, if you need a definition. We are using the word void as in abyss not as in a negation of something, although you could see it as a negation of confusion, sound and fury.

Imagine if you can sitting quietly in a forest with nothing around but the trees, or sitting by a stream where the only sound is the water and the wind or if you prefer sitting in a lovely park-like garden surrounded by nature's beauty. Drink in these moments of solitude and beauty. Feel the wind on your skin and the sun or the coolness and the spray of the water. Just allow for the simple aspects of God's creation of nature to fill your senses rather then traffic and work, and family and relationship and money and whatever. Just be in the moment, one with all that occurs naturally. You don't have to do anything to enjoy these places other than to drink them in. Then allow your Self to lose your Self in silence for a few moments. How do you feel afterward? Are you refreshed and rested? Do you feel more at ease with your Self and the world? Where has the confusion gone?

None of the time we recommend for being at peace and returning to the center of your being takes much time yet you resist because you are afraid of the silence. After you analyze what you say to your Self all day long, we believe you will find the silence a wonderful rest.

We leave you silently.
Namaste

VOID

What if your subconscious mind were like a blank white canvas that stretched for miles?

What would that feel like?

You could write or paint anything you wanted upon it or you could simply leave it blank and available. Think of a snow covered ground – one that has just had the snow finish falling. No one has walked upon it, no car has driven by. What does that invoke for you? Is it peaceful and pristine and perfect? When you meditate your goal is to have your mind become that newly fallen snow or the blank canvas.

Try to meditate and just see the flat white expanse. Sit in peace with nothing upon it, just its perfection, its undisturbed surface. Allow for nothing other than becoming one with this expanse of nothingness. For in this nothing is everything.

All possibility
All promise
All answers

are there, for there is nothing. If there is nothing, then there is nothing to push against, nothing with which you can disagree or agree, nothing to make you right or someone else wrong. It is pure life, it is pure bliss, it is simply purity. If you can get to the point of allowing for nothing during your meditation, then try to let your Self fall into the nothingness. Allow your Self to be engulfed by it. Do not be afraid for you are completely loved and supported. We are only asking you to become one with all that there is and all that there is - is nothing.

In this place you cannot be too fat, too thin, too sick, too poor, uncomfortable, unhappy or apart. For you are a part of everything when you are in the nothingness of life. We hope that you can achieve these moments of pure bliss and freedom. We know it is foreign to you, but if you trust (ah there is the word) that you can float in nothing and be surrounded in love then you will find the bliss you desire.

We leave in bliss and love.

Namaste

PAIN

How many of you are in pain? Now this does not have to mean physical pain, but rather mental, physical, Spiritual, psychic anguish. How long have you been in pain? Do you even realize that you are in pain or has it become so familiar that you believe this is the natural course of things?

Let us take the obvious physical pain first. Where do you hurt? Is there a reason for the pain or ache or discomfort? If there is, what have you done about improving your situation? Do you believe that you can find relief from the pain or have you been "told" there is nothing you can do? How much do you allow the pain to affect your normal daily life? Do you ignore pain or do you embrace it or do you live somewhere in-between? Could it be caused by food or other things you do? How do you mask the pain - with medication, alcohol, food or anger? Think about this for a few moments for it is important to know how you treat the pain. Do you push it away, do you ignore it, do you embrace it or do you try to ameliorate it?

Now let us move to mental anguish. How much pain is there in your thoughts? How painful is your daily life because of these thoughts? Are you uplifting and loving in your thoughts about your Self? If not, why not? Are you not a child of God? Do you not deserve joy and love and abundance and peace? If you do not, why is that so? If you were to ask those that love you if you deserved joy what would they say? Now how do you medicate this pain? Do you run from it or do you bravely wade into the fray and fight the demons and remove them so that you can have peace of mind?

What is Spiritual pain? It can manifest in many ways. Many of you have been pushed away from embracing the Spirituality that is truly yours because of early experiences within organized religion. You carry great guilt, fear, anger and upset within you from what you were told was "true" about God. Many of you can't even hear the word God without cringing or trying to find another word. Why is this? What is the pain of finding God – Goodness? How can this hurt you? What is wrong in finding inner peace and connection to something that is greater than this life, something that will lift you up and set you free? Why stop your Self from connecting with something that lives within you and can be accessed at will. How do you treat Spiritual pain?

Psyche pain is very similar to mental and Spiritual pain, but with slight shadings. It is more of the sum total of the two but the sum is greater than the parts. Most of you experience this on some level. It makes you feel alone, apart, lonely, afraid and scared. It is the disconnection from source, from the light of God's world and from the connection within each of you that has the ability to tap into the source of enlightenment. It is available to you all and yet you remain locked in worlds of judgment, darkness and fear. We offer that the pain can be erased with a steady practice of coming into silence and communion. Working to find the bliss within and the void for as we have said before.....

Within the nothing is everything.

We leave in perfection and wholeness.
Namaste

WILLFULNESS

How important is it to be right? How important is it to be "in control?" How does control work for you? What does control buy you or give you? How often do you do something that is not in your true best interest just to "prove" that you are in control?

Think about this in your personal relationships. Do you want to control other people's behaviours? Do you want to control the outcome of the situation or of most situations? Are you willing to allow that there might be a myriad of other ways to reach a solution to a problem or is there only one way – yours? What does it cost you emotionally, physically or even financially to maintain this control? And now the most important question – Are you really in control or are you simply controlling the moment or event in front of you? Is the control real or is it imagined?

Control rarely works over the long haul. It may work in a specific situation and it may work for a long time in your reality, but in the end you will find that most other humans do not want to be controlled. They too want to have free will and freedom to make decisions about their life and their circumstances. In the end this leads to unhappy interpersonal relationships. Most of you justify it that you "know" the best outcome and maybe you do – for you. Is it really possible to know what is best for another person? Do you know where their journey must take them? We know that it is often very difficult to allow people you love or care about to make their own decisions because often those decisions take them away from you in some way, but the key is that they are their decisions. Life has many roads to explore and you can only take so many in any one life time so the choices are endless.

Fear is what is behind control. It is behind all control even though it may look more like anger or power or other dominating energies. Control puts your life in what appears to be a neatly ordered box, a safe and contained space that is not too big and not too small for you to control. Then you begin to put people and events and things inside the box so that they too can be safe from all harm and fears. It does not work this way because the walls of this controlled environment are subject to breaching at anytime because other people have their own fear controlled worlds that will collide with yours and create havoc and dismay. Now, the havoc and dismay that is created is not really real, but it will seem that way to you the more you attempt to control the breech. If you allow that your life is a continuum with no ability to see the future then you will find that your grasping onto what is "real" will lessen and you will begin to glide along your life rather than go kicking, screaming and grasping your way through.

Please sit with this lesson for a few days and watch as you begin to believe you can control something. Begin to notice the difference between putting in your input and knowledge and then allowing for the outcome. Sometimes the "allowed" outcome is far better than the controlled outcome for it exceeds your expectation. Sometimes it appears to be not what you want or think it should be, but with some time and history you might be able to see that it was, in the end, the perfect solution.

We leave you with open hands and hearts.
Namaste

CENTERED

How centered are you?

Do you feel strongly that the core of your being is firmly rooted and unable to be blown about by the winds of fortune?

How susceptible are you to stress, upset, chaos?

Do you remain calm and unaffected during times of high stress or are you joining in with others in the frenetic pace of life?

Stop and think about the last time you felt stress. Was it yours? By this we mean did you take a situation and allow your Self to become so involved with its outcome that it became a stress to you? Did you feel nervous, overworked, unable to focus, unable to believe that you could easily and calmly reach your goal? Did you cause the stress or were the stressors around you and you simply joined in? Again, sit and think of the most glaring stress situation you can. It may be occurring now or in the past or it could even be something you are anticipating. Who or what is causing the stress? If it is you - Why? What do you derive from being worn out, exhausted, unhappy, angry and on edge? How will this condition change the outcome? Will your stress allow you to make better decisions? Is there any need for the stress? What if you calmly evaluated the situation and looked for the solutions. What if you simply continued on your path of living or work and allowed the “stressors” to fall by the way as you simply negotiated the path of life?

Now we are not saying that others don’t appear in life and share their stress with you? They most certainly do, for they too want others to feel the unease and exhaustion, but is it your problem – their stress? In a situation whether it be work or personal other people can come to you and insist that their work, needs, problems take precedent over yours. Maybe their issues do, but it is always in your choice to put aside your journey to assist and if you choose to set aside your needs for that time period why must it create stress? It is your choice to do it stressfully or with calm. Which sounds better?

The key to living fully and joyfully and well is to remove the "musts" and "cannots" and "impossibles" from your vocabulary and replace them with "could be," "maybe," "might" for in these words lies peace and possibility. Always put your eye on the ultimate goal and then allow your Self to walk as quietly, peacefully and calmly as you can toward that outcome. Running there in a panic won't change the outcome, but it will exhaust you and then you will not have the energy to rationally move in the direction you choose. Save your strength through peaceful living.

We leave quietly and in love.
Namaste

SORROW

This is a pervasive energy on your planet. There is an underlying sorrow that permeates your existence. One that looks for the things that are wrong or sad or painful or depressing. It is as though you believe that all human condition is about suffering and sadness. Please take a moment to look at the continuum of your life. You can pick a one year period or a five year period or you can sit in analysis of your entire life, it does not matter. The more time you analyze the larger your perspective.

Now the difficult part of this exercise is that you must separate your perception and "you" from this observation. By "you" we mean your beliefs, your stories, and your emotions for we want you to be an observer not a participant. First, think of the things that have been sad or difficult or depressing or lonely. Now don't think of them as you would as "you," but rather look at the time period you have chosen and pick out the sad, bad, unhappy, difficult things. Write them down and assign a time to them. Did it last an hour, a day, a week, a month, months or years? Be honest. Again do not think or write down how long you allowed it to affect "you," but rather how long was the event or incident. Now write down the joyful, happy, loving moments in the same time period. Again, do not attach to the emotion, but rather just observe.

When this is complete, take the two lists and add up the time. How much of the time period you chose was used up in the combination of emotions? Which emotion is the more dominant? We would guess that it is the sadness, sorrow and despair for you seem to believe that this is the most acceptable place to choose for your life story. Very few of you focus on what works, on the joy, the possibility and the laughter of your life. You miss the love and the excitement because you are mired down in the perspective that life is hard and full of pain and difficulty. All lives have difficulty and all lives have joy but it is the fire you chose to fan that matters. Do you attach to joy or to sorrow?

We would like you to sit with this lesson for some time. Think about the stories you tell your Self. Notice the choices you make during the day that kick you out of happiness or simply peace and put you in upset and anger and sorrow. We envision a world for you that is full of possibilities, love, laughter, joy and living. What do you envision?

We leave you in joy.
Namaste

POSSIBILITY

How open are you to unlimited possibilities?

Are you willing to believe that that if you miss the possibility bus you had hoped for that there will be another one along any minute? Most of you think that there is a finite number. Only four or five wonderful things could possibly happen in your life and so you carefully pick the things you want to happen. You plan and control the outcome. You shape your life, your education, your friends, even the place you live around these things that you have determined are "possible." They are precious jewels to you and so you guard them and hope for them and wait for them, but you are often waiting for them at the "Controlled Possibility Terminal" of the bus station. While you sit on your lonely bench and wait, there are all sorts of buses of possibility zooming by, stopping right outside your door, idling waiting for you to notice, but you don't because they are not the bus you want or think you need.

Get on the BUS OF LIFE! If you are on the bus it is moving and you are going somewhere. Most of you are waiting for the "right" bus to come along with all your dreams on board and so you wait. If you grabbed a bus going by and began the ride called LIFE you would be seeing all sorts of opportunities and possibilities you never imagined. You could be talking to your other "bus mates" and finding out where they are going or what connections they are making. Maybe you have not ridden many buses in your life, but here's a big secret. If you continue to go in a forward direction to the end of the line they will issue you unlimited transfers. Yes, you can always transfer off the bus you are on and onto another one that might be going to a new and more exciting location.

Many of you find this concept foreign and want to get off the bus and cross over to take a bus back in the opposite direction. You want to go back to the past or stay exactly where you are. What is in the past that is so much more exciting than the future, than continuing your life's journey? Did you leave people, a job or something back there that you believe if you retrieve it your life will work again and once you pick it or them up and bring it forward into *this* life; things will be "fine?" Life is always lived forward; the past can come as memories, but it is all they can provide. Life is what is happening while you are making plans and while you are trying to control the outcome. All sorts of wonderful changes are occurring in every moment and you have to just be willing to look for them to find that life is possible and joyful and action packed. It is a ride of a lifetime. Enjoy it.

We ask you to pack this meditation up, climb on the BUS OF LIFE and think about it as you ride into your future.

We leave in excitement.
Namaste

DEDICATION

How willing are you to stay on the path? Once you have chosen a route to some goal or desire do you stay the course to reach your goal? What if there is not immediate evidence that it is working or that it is the right path? What if the road is hard or it takes years longer than planned? Do you continue with single-minded determination or do you just give up?

Now some may say that this is contradictory to our other teachings in that we are asking if you continue on a path toward something with no evidence it is the right path. Life is not about absolutes. It is not about right and wrong and good or bad, it is about experience. If you set your mind toward accomplishing something then how committed are you to the completion is our question?

Let us take exercise. Do you exercise? Do you do it regularly, intermittently, maniacally or never? Are there spurts of exertion followed by months or years of inertia? Do you have to exercise everyday or life is not worth living? There is no one right answer, there are many ways to moving your body, but if you make a commitment to exercise or tone your body, do you stick to it? Are you willing to stay the course?

This can be applied to school, weight, jobs, relationships - actually any aspect of your life. What we want you to observe is your personality traits. Maybe some of you never stick to any one plan; others never give up any plan even if all evidence points to it being a bad idea and others drop in and out of determination. They can be very determined about something and very lackadaisical about others.

The assignment here is to take an inventory of what matters to you. What are you willing to commit to and stay committed?

Look at friendships, relationships, jobs, your health, your Spirituality and connection with others. Which ones seem to be easy to do and which ones seem harder or more arduous or not worth it at all? This will help you to assess your Self in an honest and true light and give you some relief from beating your Self up about certain areas of your life. Take your inventory, look at your "hot spots" that might need work and begin the work.

We leave you with determination.
Namaste

ENERGY

Do you feel energized, full of energy, ready to take on whatever life brings your way?

Do you feel that you can create your own energy or do you think that it is something you either have or do not have?

Think about a time in which you were tired and felt exhausted and then something else occurred to remove your mind from your exhaustion – perhaps a friend stopped by or you laughed or something engaged you in the moment. The next thing you knew it was much later and you were not feeling tired at all. Energy is available to you in all moments of life. Just as adrenalin can hit your system in times of stress, so can energy be tapped into. The key is that you must be willing to feel energized.

Exhaustion is caused by all the same things that cause everything else – body, mind and Spirit. What makes it easy to work long, hard days sometimes and on others to want to quit after a few moments? Depression causes exhaustion, stress causes exhaustion; loneliness is also a factor. You can exhaust your Self through hard work and exertion, but what can you do about it? We would suggest working on your mental ability to find the joy, the laughter, the peace and tranquility that is yours from meditation and insight. You can derive more energy from five minutes of meditation than you can from a fitful night's sleep. It is in the calming of your being - your total being - that you feel more alive and in tune and energized.

Do you work too hard mentally? By this we mean do you constantly have thoughts running through your head, things you "must" do, things happening? Do you allow for down time, do you allow for periods of silence and meditation? Can you be at peace?

If you can find the peace, the pace of life will slow immeasurably and yet it will also begin to accelerate in ways you could not imagine. Sit with these concepts for a bit and analyze how you use your energy and your thoughts and your time and then take a few moments to look inward to the peace at the center of your being.

We leave in love and peace.
Namaste

CHAOS

How chaotic is your life right now?

Do you feel out of control and balance?

Do you feel that everything that has been is no longer?

Do you fear that you will not know how
to live in the new life?

Are you concerned that everything has changed
and nothing will remain the same?

Do not despair. There are always times of great upheaval in life. Changes occur in relationships, jobs, health, friendships, finances and belief systems. There is the reordering of family dynamics as children grow up and leave, people pass away and change occurs. Chaos is a constant state and it is, by nature, uncontrollable, but how you handle your Self, your fears and your changes is completely under your control.

Have you ever felt that you were standing in a room full of people and no one can hear or see you? Do you feel misunderstood or abandoned? Why? Have you abandoned your Self? Have you left or is it that the whirl of life around you is not familiar any longer? Change can be chaotic. Discovery of who you are can cause the waters of your life to be roiled up and therefore seem unfamiliar, but again DO NOT DESPAIR. *YOU*, the essence of you is still intact.

Take a few moments right now to sit down and just center your Self. Take several deep, cleansing breaths – each time saying to your Self, “All is Calm. All is just as it should be.” Just breathe in slowly through your nose and out through your mouth. Ask for peace. Attempt to take your Self to complete silence, to just no chatter at all inside your head. If it helps you could imagine that you are listening to water as in a stream or the ocean or just a pool lapping on the sides. If another image of nature calms you, put that in your time of peace. Just allow and sit for a few moments. It may seem like an eternity, but you can do it. Honor the silence. Get rid of the "Sturm und Drang" and be calm and at peace. Sit as long as you need to or can. Try this a couple of times per day or as often as you need it during times of great stress. It is only a moment or so we are asking and it will help to remind you that there is always calm at the eye of the storm, so if the chaos is surrounding you, become the eye and live peacefully as it swirls about you.

Remember that at the center of your being is peace. It is the core of who you are. The rest of the craziness or noise or stress or sadness or whatever is troubling you right now is outside of you. Travel to the center of your Self and find the blessed silence.

We leave in peace and calm.
Namaste

PITY

Do you pity your Self?

Do you feel sorry for all the tribulations, trials, upsets and chaos you perceive to be in your life?

Do you look around at other people and their lives and feel that somehow your life is less than theirs?

Do you feel overburdened?

Do you take on jobs, activities, responsibilities and then hope that others "notice" how wonderful, busy, overworked or over-burdened you are?

If you answer *YES* to any of these questions there is most likely a sliver of pity going on.

Life is about choice. You don't always get to choose the events of your lives or how they come out. Often they do not match your ideas of what you want or wish, but that does not mean that the experience is not good for you. More importantly, it could be good for your Soul for that is the point of this life. What is your Soul getting from this thing called life? Is it getting the lessons it craves, desires or needs? It is nearly impossible for you to answer that question, for very few of you know what your Soul truly needs. Your Soul lives in a wonderful place of peace and bliss most of the time. The daily chaos and turmoil of living does not necessarily touch your Soul as it does your physical being. The worst day of your life could be the best one for your Soul and its journey, which is why being grateful for all of life's experiences moves you forward more rapidly through life.

Often it is the challenges, the roadblocks or the huge mountains of humanity that cause you truly to have the most growth. It is the losses, the upsets, the trials and tribulations that strengthen you and help you move toward freedom from human constraints. Please do not misunderstand we are not saying that you should attract unhappiness or chaos, but rather that when it occurs you need to embrace the experience, move through it in a forward direction and continue on the journey. Most of you get stuck in the eddy of turmoil. Something difficult occurs, you lose a loved one for example and you stay in the grieving and sadness and loss for way too long. Their Soul is set free, but yours remains trapped in the past, the "might have beens," the sorrow and the loss. If the death occurred because of a tragedy or at the hand of someone else or war, it is easy to stay mired in the loss. You have been robbed, in essence, of their love, but we ask if that is really true? You have been robbed of their physical presence, but not their love. You have lost a daily physical companion but not a Soul mate. Your Soul does not "lose" things as you perceived you do as a human, so it is not the same.

The key to living a life fulfilled; and by that we mean a life that fills your Spirit and Soul with joy; is to experience the moments you are given in this life, feeling the emotions that are attached to them, but always keep moving forward. Move through the pain, the upset, the sorrow as well as moving through the joy, the happiness and the elation. Here is a question. When something wonderful happens to you and you are ecstatic, do you carry that ecstasy, that joy forward with you? Do you stay stuck in the joy? When something difficult occurs do you say, "Oh I can't experience that because I am so joyful?" Now think about something sad - When something happy happens are you stuck in the sadness, in the pity of loss or do you embrace the joy, laugher and gaiety? Is your response to express the joy from your place of sorrow or to say, "I can't be happy because I am so sad?" Sit with this juxtaposition for awhile. See how you rob your Self often of joy and happiness while you choose to wallow in sadness and despair, because in the end you all want the pity more than the ecstasy.

We leave you in contemplation.
Namaste

CONFUSION

What confuses you most?
What conundrums in your life have you most baffled?
What is it you want to know?

Most of the time that you become confused or befuddled or cloudy in your thinking is during times of great stress. Now the decisions you may be trying to make may be ones that are happy or good or further your life in some way that is pleasant to you, but still the process of choosing has stress. Is this right or wrong? Is this best for me? If it is something that you truly believe that you desire then it is difficult to be as objective since you want the outcome to be a certain way. If the outcome does not play out in your preconceived way it becomes a disappointment, but we offer that you should try to allow the outcome to be neutral. Can you really know what is best for you? Think of an event that went exactly as you had planned or wished. The outcome matched the result. Now do a short analysis of that entire scenario. Was it all positive? Were there some rough spots? Did it completely match your pictures for the entire occurrence? Did it start well, but then become something that was not quite as you imagined? Again we want to remind you that life is a constant flow and that there is nothing static about the process, even if you wish it to be.

Now, think about a time an event did not turn out as hoped. Was it as devastating in reality as it was in your mind? What new paths did it lead you down? What new people, opportunities or life moments occurred in place of the one imagined? Were you able to appreciate the new, unplanned gifts or were you too focused on the loss of your "picture" in your head that you didn't notice that other things filled in the gaps.

When you are upset or confused by something, simply take the time to sit with it for a while. Get quiet and at peace with your Self. Then sit and allow your Self to put the question into the silence. Try not to allow this question or decision to roil around in the silence you have created, but rather just ask that it be included and then attempt to make your mind quiet again. At the end of this time you will feel greater clarity about the issue. Your thoughts may have changed in ways you didn't think possible or you may simply find your Self calmer about the event in question. Always remember to breathe and you will be fine.

We leave you in clarity.
Namaste

LOSS

What have you lost?
What is missing that you long for?
Is there a part of you that never seems to fill up?
Is there a pervasive sadness that you don't understand?

For many it is easy to find things that are lost to them. It could be the death of a loved one, a job, a home, friends, pets or a way of life? For some it could be their health. For many however, there is a sense of loss or something missing in their lives and when they try to analyze the situation, they come up somewhat empty. Most of their life seems to be working and for someone else it would be a happy life, but it is not for them. What is missing? One answer is "Self." How in control of your Self do you feel? Now we have spoken many times about how life is not in your control and this is very true, but your possession of Self is within your control. Who are you? What do you want? Why can't you be happy? For many, these questions haunt you or exhaust you or trouble you in some way. How do you find your Self? How do you reclaim you?

The first steps are to journey within. This is terrifying to most because they do not know what is in there and for many they are fearful they will not like what they find. Isn't that fascinating that you are most afraid of your Self? What is so dark and foreboding about traveling to the core of your Self to discover who you are and what you want? You claim to long to know – "If I only knew what I was to be when I grow up?" – yet you do not want to do the work. It is better to stay mad at your parents, siblings, spouses, friends and the circumstances of life rather than to take a journey of Self-discovery.

Are you willing to give up being a victim of the outside world and become the commander of the interior life? If your answer is yes or even maybe, you can start that journey right now. Sit quietly in meditation. Again, do not be put off by that word, it simply means that for five or ten or twenty minutes you sit with a blank mind, a canvas if you will, upon which you can see the movies of your life, the paintings of your world, the music of your Soul. You can inhabit the grace that is always available to you. In times of great chaos you have a shelter with you at all times, YOU. There is great peace, joy and love available to you, from you, with all your love, always. YOU - and you carry it everywhere you go, every day of your life and most of you don't even know it exists.

Think about the life you have now. Think about how you feel loss or lost and then think about a life with joy, light and laughter. Which do you choose, for it is always your choice!

We leave in laughter.
Namaste

ALLOWING

How willing are you to allow things to happen in your life? By this we mean how willing are you to let go of the control, the fear, the worry, the planning and just allow? We are not suggesting a life of no structure, for structure is a necessary part of living. We are not advocating chaos in the sense of a wildly, out of control existence, but rather we are suggesting that your barriers to joy be removed so that you may more fully experience your life.

Now, some of you will say that you are living in the moment and that you are fully in life, but we ask you to rethink your position. If your life is not working as you wish and you believe that you are "allowing" for all possibility to enter your life, we ask you to rethink this position. Sit quietly for a moment and think about a life that is abundant, full of excitement, adventure, love and joy. Now, simply notice as you read that sentence what happens to your body – does it tense up, does it feel uncomfortable anywhere? Are your shoulders relaxed and at ease - your hands and fingers? Are you clenched anywhere? Now here is the sentence again, think about your thoughts as you read it.

"Think about a life that is abundant, full of excitement, adventure, love and joy."

If you listen carefully, are there any comments of disbelief? Do you think, "Well, I am allowing and I am ready for fabulous things and nothing happens?" Do you believe, truly, honestly and deeply, that good things can happen to you? Maybe you think that they "should" happen or wish that they "would" happen, but do you *believe* they will?

Okay, take this a step further, when something wonderful happens do you rejoice fully in it or is there another voice in your head that says, “Careful, it won’t last” or “You don’t deserve that” or “What happens if I don’t live up to whatever?” Listen to the Self-sabotage that occurs. The problem with it is that it is insidious and you have trained your Self to not listen to the subtlety of your inner voices, but rather to the broader picture that you present to the world. Allow your Self to be honest with your Self. Listen to the judgment, fear, upset and disbelief. Do not be afraid of it for if you bring it out into the open and sit with it, some of the “boogey man” feeling of those beliefs will begin to dissipate and you can begin to relieve your Self of their power.

So we ask you to take the time, maybe fifteen minutes a day, to sit with your negative beliefs and begin to dispel them so that you will be able to fully allow the glory of this life to fill the spaces of your existence.

We leave you in love and peace.
Namaste

KINDNESS

How kind are you?

Is it conditional?

Does it come with strings or a price?

Are you naturally kind or do you have to make an effort to extend your Self to others?

Do you willingly accept kindness that is passed to you by others?

What is kindness? For many it is simply the act of extending their Self to do something or listen or share their time. For others it is Selfless acts of their time, money, person and Spirit. Kindness is a form of intimacy and many of you are walled off from your fellow man so you do not feel that you can be universally kind. Kindness really is nothing more than being completely in the moment with another human being. It is listening, observing and caring that in the moment that you are together there is a connection. Even if the person is annoying or ill-behaved, it does not rob you of anything to be kind and gentle in your experience of them. Kindness is living without walls or boundaries or conditions. It is about being available.

How kind are you to your Self? Do you lift your Self up with gentle remarks? Do you forgive your Self for your daily foibles, missteps and poor time management? Do you allow that you are human and therefore fallible? At the end of the day are you willing to look at the day with gentle eyes and state it was a day well lived – even if you didn't finish all your work or didn't call the friends you were meant to call? If you were curt or unkind to others, can you forgive your Self and simply make a promise to try harder the next day to be less irritable, or stressed or overloaded? Can you forgive your procrastination to get things done? Forgiveness and kindness go hand in hand. Take a few moments today to think about acts of kindness that you can perform. Were any of those acts for you?

Kindness starts at home and with Self. Practice on your Self for a while and then see if you can then roll out the acts of kindness into the world - for if you can experience it always with your Self it will be always available to others.

We leave you gently and with love.
Namaste

WASTE

How much time do you waste each day? Now we are not asking you to be judgmental about things you choose to do when you "should" be doing something else, but rather we are asking from a perspective of – "What do you spend your thoughts on?" Do your thoughts move you forward; are they uplifting and positive? Do your thoughts enliven and excite you and bring you joy? How much of your day is spent worrying that you have offended someone or that they have offended you? Do you stay stuck in the minutia of life about all the things you think matter? In the end of a life does it truly matter that the wash was completed in that day or moment or that someone cleaned their room or that a report was completed for work? Do most things hinge on life and death or is there some room in your life to set aside the day-to-day requirements and just be at peace with your Self?

Yes, we are back on the topic of peace within for it is the key to everything else. Some of you might think this redundant as we have "covered" this before, but we say that we have not even scratched the surface of what we mean by being peaceful within. Every moment you spend worrying about the outcome of something or replaying the outcome and trying to figure out how you could have changed the outcome when it is already decided is wasted time. It is what it is - Nothing more and nothing less. Life is a series of moments but if you stay stuck too long in any one of them you step out of life and into your head. It is very hard to be alive in your head for life is happening outside of you. Be in action.

If someone has left you whether through death or attrition of the relationship, can you bring them back with thoughts? Can you change the outcome? If they are still alive do you really want them back or do you simply want the familiarity? If they have transitioned out of life is there anything you can do to change that outcome? The answer to both situations is that you can only control how your react to the "loss." Life is transition. Life is flux. Life is change. It is not static but you all want to waste hours, days, weeks, months and years wondering what "might have been" or wishing for a different outcome.

Life is like a coin toss – it is either heads or tails. You can always toss the coin again and again and again, but each toss is a separate act, not the cumulative "two out of three." Maybe the coin toss is right and you are wrong since you enjoy putting life in such simple terms. Take the journey you are on and stop wasting your time sitting waiting for a different itinerary.

Get about living and stop wasting your time, talent, energy and love on "might have been's" and "wish it were's." Live and laugh and enjoy the ride.

We leave in joy and laughter.
Namaste

CONNECTION

Stop and think for a moment about the interconnections of your life. If you are old enough, think about the times in life that you have seen people that you have not seen in years and how that allows you to see them differently. Perhaps they were people that in the past had seemed difficult or superior or not available. Now you meet again years later and they seem approachable or humble or open to relationship. Why is this so? Have they changed? Have you?

We allow our personal drama, insecurity, beliefs and controls to color our relationships. We judge other people based on our personality in that moment not necessarily theirs. Our ability to connect is colored by us much of the time. Think about someone that you have met recently that you found to be less than approachable. What was it about them that kept you from feeling connected? Was it their demeanor, their attitude, their position, their status, their education, their money? What was it that caused you to be put off or to feel unable to approach?

Think of a co-worker that is particularly prickly. What comes to mind? What do you "think" is "their" problem? Take a moment or two to sit and relax as you think about them. Allow your mind to let go of what you believe and just sit with this person's image before you. Think compassionate thoughts about the person. If they are particularly difficult simply send them compassionate, loving thoughts that they might be in peace. Do not try to analyze them or their behaviour; just be in peace with them in your thoughts. That is the entire exercise. There is nothing more to do. Connection is about you letting down your barriers to communication. Other people can keep theirs up and keep you away, but the more you allow your barriers to be down the happier and more connected you will feel.

Now we want you to understand the purpose of this exercise; it is to give you peace and calm in a situation. As you begin to let go of your resistance, you begin to feel more connected with others. This does not mean that you become everyone's best friend or that you allow your Self to be used or abused by difficult people. Rather we are saying if your barriers are down and you can be available to communicate in an open and loving and caring way, relationship with others can be transformed. If people have less to resist or push against it allows them to become calm and move to peace and love.

We leave you in love.
Namaste

LOVE

How often do you allow your Self to stop and feel love? Just simple, heart-filling love! There doesn't have to be a person you direct this feeling towards, for love is not external. Love is universal and internal and external and all inclusive and magnificent and available to each of you in any moment, but how many of you allow it to bloom in your hearts? When was the last time you allowed your Self to have the glow of love in your system?

For most of you it is a conditional thing that comes to you from the outside. You wait and wait and wait for love to come your way. You wait to feel loved. You wait to find love. You long for love. You claim that love is out there somewhere and you want to find it. You think you are unlovable.

What is love? Some of you think it is sex or you are willing to substitute sex for love. Some think it is money or food or alcohol or drugs. Yes, that is where you think these wonderful feelings lie so you misuse them in the hopes of "feeling" good enough while masking the feelings with these crutches.

Stop for a moment and think about love. What do you think it is? How does it feel? Do you allow those feelings? Love seems to be very "push me/pull me" for many of you. You long for it and for the intimacy of the love, yet you push it away when it shows up. Why? What would happen if you allowed for love to fill you up? Is it not to be trusted? Is it dangerous? It is only love. You are the ones that put all the conditions upon love. It has to be this way and from this person and it must meet all these conditions before it is "right." Many of you have decided to withhold love from people because they don't deserve it or you don't deserve it. You can honestly love everyone on this planet just as they are right now. They do not have to do anything to deserve love nor do you. They only have to allow for it to happen.

Loving someone doesn't require that you do anything except remove the walls to connection. You can send loving thoughts to every driver that makes you angry rather than sending the disgust and anger you send now. You don't have to speak to them or know their name or ever see them again, but if you send love rather than hate you begin to fill your Self up with joy rather than sadness. Maybe it is a form of compassion, maybe it is just a way to make your life fuller and happier and full of joy rather than sadness, depression, judgment and hate.

Think of a dog and how they faithfully send you love and warmth with no expectation. Even when you are not kind to them, they usually respond with loving eyes, a wagging tail and a hope for a better, loving moment.

We leave you with the hope that you will allow your Self to experience love for a time today. Try it on your Self first. Practice on you. Think a loving thought or two about who you are and just allow it to be. Replace your judgment with love and see how it feels.

We leave you in hope.
Namaste

CONFUSION

Does it ever seem that you take two steps forward and one back? That you are going on a path toward a goal and then huge roadblocks are thrown up and "seem" to keep you from your goal? Are these roadblocks Self-imposed or are they placed there by "evil forces" or other aspects?

Think about a recent time in which you were moving along a path that seemed to be open and had clear sailing. All the things were working and you were excited that you were heading in the right direction. Now these feeling of success and no barriers may have only lasted a day or it could have been days, weeks, months or even years. Then "suddenly" it all became more difficult or harder or more complicated or it seemed that no matter where you looked or turned there was chaos where once had reigned contentment and joy. What was your reaction to this change in energy? Did you feel puzzled, put upon, discouraged, outraged, sad, angry or just confused?

Please take the time to analyze your emotions around this problem or change in the course of your life. It is important to understand how it made you feel or how it is making you feel right now. Sometimes things change for a very good reason. It may be that your time with this project is done, it maybe that this job, relationship, whatever no longer suits you. The hard part is that you do not know why. Humans want to know why. You want to know why you are being tormented or treated badly when you have been so loyal, faithful, loving, caring, hard-working or whatever the thoughts are about the situation. Maybe it is just time for you to be done. Maybe it is a test of your determination to keep moving through the chaos into clarity. All we can tell you is to do the best you can in a situation. Be who you are and let the chips fall where they may. Continue to be the best YOU that you know how to be and to live your life in integrity and caring about the outcome. If you can, sit with the situation for a short while and truly analyze where you are with the process. How to heart are you taking others judgments? How to heart are you taking that this is happening to you rather than it is simply happening. Sit with your Soul for a while and feel what is best for you.

The key when you are confused is to sit with your Self because initially you will be sitting in the box you have created called LIFE. That box is yours and yours alone. It has been created by you. Many of you feel that you control the box, but maybe the box controls you because while you are sitting in the box, life is happening all around you. As life happens around you the box is going to get blown back and forth, passersby are going to kick or hit or touch the box of your life in ways you would prefer to not have happen. They are going to jostle the box of your life. One way to avoid the discomfort and confusion of this constant parade by your sacred box is to expand the boundaries of it to include the chaos and the confusion and the not knowing and to embrace the sea of living that streams by you daily. Allow for chaos and it will have less effect.

We leave you full of possibility and chaos.
Namaste

CHAOS

It is a time of great chaos and many people feel off balance and out of control. Life is happening at a very fast pace and changes come upon you quickly. If you are not willing to have the changes occur than it may seem that life is very topsy turvey right now and that you have very little control over the outcomes of your life.

Is this really true? Yes and no are the answers. You are living in times that are fast moving. Your communications move rapidly, you are rarely out of touch with one another or society; there is very little time for leisure and peace. How willing are you to step out of the chaos and just be at peace? Now this is a frightening thought for many of you because you believe that if you are not in the middle of the fast moving water called life that you will be left behind, but we offer that there are many ways to float down the river of life and each has merit. Right now if your life seems like a lot of white water and turbulence and dangerous obstacles to avoid that may be very well true. How exhilarating do you find that life? Is it life affirming to you? Do you derive energy from the chaotic aspects of it? Do you feel that you are mastering it by riding these roiling waters and still being afloat? Does the adrenalin keep you feeling alive? Or does it exhaust you and leave you worried, tired and concerned? Do you sleep well and find rest in your quiet times? Do you allow for your quiet times?

We offer to you that there is a quiet stream that flows along the same path and can even lead to many of the same places, but the path of that stream is smoother, calmer and contains fewer obstacles. It is not that it is a river of no challenges, but rather they are met with peace rather than dramas of conquering the obstacles. All lives contain obstacles to overcome, the choice is do you travel at such a pace that they surprise you and require immediate action to avoid injury or would you prefer to have a slower approach that allows you to prepare a bit better? Life happens in every moment. There are good/bad, easy/hard, happy/sad, triumphant and defeating moments in all lives. It is your reaction to them; it is your approach that creates your life.

So take a moment to think about the speed of your life. Are you running white water most of the time or do you have a combination of fast moving and pastoral waters? Can you allow your Self the peace so that you can take time to move down the tributaries of life into less exhilarating waters that allow you peace and joy in the journey? Are you willing to take time to be simply at peace with your Self and those closest to you? Do you take time to sit with people that are close that perhaps cannot handle the normal crazy pace of your life? Can you sit for five minutes in quiet and meditation and feel that it has been time well spent? We offer to you that taking those five minutes or more per day will take much of the chaos in your life and put it into perspective and into joy.

We leave you quietly in peace.
Namaste

LOVE

What is it?

What does it look like?

Is it scarce or is there an abundance?

Do you allow for it to enter your life fully,
without boundaries?

Is it finite or infinite?

What does it require of you?

What is to be feared?

Love is a complex discussion about a very simple emotion. Love is a flowing of energy that knows no bounds. It is an infinite river. It is the river of life. Love is the element that most seek and many seek fruitlessly throughout their lives. They learn early on that love is conditional and elusive. They feel unloved or unlovable. They create walls to love because they feel that it is easier to keep love out than let it in. "Love hurts" is a phrase used by many of you. Does it? The answer is no. Love does not hurt. Love is the calming energy of peace and abundance. It is the absence of love that hurts and many of you set it up so that you have the Self-fulfilling prophecy that love is something that you can lose so you must hold on as tightly as you can. Love is not a bus that comes by once. It comes by every moment of every day but most of you cannot access it. You want to meter it out from your own being and you do not trust others to love you "enough" or love you "the right way." What is the right way?

The problems begin when you put love in human terms. It instantly becomes conditional for most humans. It is about loving you IF. Love is not about IF; it is about love that is all. Love is an act of kindness done without thought in the moment. Love is about caring for another human or animal or thing without any thought to your Self or your needs in that moment. Love is picking up the phone and calling someone to tell them you are thinking of them. Love is offering a shoulder, a safe place or your hand in friendship. Love occurs in the small moments of life. Love could be as simple as allowing someone to go in front of you in a line at the store because in that moment you show compassion, you show connection, you cared enough to notice that they have a short order and you could easily wait for them.

Do not limit love. Do not parcel it out as though you only have so much to give and share with this planet. This is not a scary concept because we are not asking you to run out and hug strangers or take them into your homes if you are not so motivated. We are simply suggesting that if you remove some of your walls to connection with others you will begin to feel the connectedness of the human race. As you begin to feel that you will begin to feel love. Love is connection, love is grand, love is compassion. If others do not accept the love you share that is their loss not yours. Do not expect any like for like return; just know that as it flows out it will return. Let go of the expectation and live in the moment of giving out your supply. It is like the Horn of Plenty, there is an unending source of love within you. Access it so that the front of your love flow doesn't begin to solidify like a lava cap, but rather keeps moving ever outward into the world in the hopes that peace and harmony can become the norm rather than the despair, dissent and unrest in which you now live.

We leave fully in love.
Namaste

FOOD

How do you relate to food?

Is it a friendly relationship?

Is it one that nourishes you, giving you energy and strength or is it adversarial and difficult?

Your society is awash in beliefs about food and diet. Eat only this or don't eat that or eat this way or that way and you will have the perfect health and vitality. Be a vegetarian, eat only fish, eat raw meat or eat only fruit. Eat high fiber or low fat or no carbohydrates. Never eat sugar. What is right? Are you confused by all this input and information? Why?

Most of you do not have a normal relationship with fueling your body. Food is love or food is comfort or food is an enemy or can't be eaten under stress or can only be eaten in huge quantities under stress. Sit for a minute and think about your relationship with food. For some this is an easy task for food permeates their thoughts. They fantasize about what they love to eat or what they are going to eat. Others just find whatever is available and stuff it into their faces without thought to how it truly tastes or what it is doing to their body. Some despair that they will never be thin or in tune with food. Others never think about food, they forget to eat. Others live on sugar and still others obsess about each gram and morsel that they consume.

So think about your relationship. What do you do with food? First of all think of how you think of food. Is it a friend or a thing or an enemy? Next just sit with your feelings about the topic of food and diet. What emotions come up for you? List those emotions – they can range from joy and ecstasy; to frustration and anger. Think about a variety of your lessons or feelings about food for your relationship can run the gamut of emotions from joy to anger. If you are neutral about food does that make you happy? Neutrality is the best place to be for then you can be in any state of nourishment and be at peace. If you LOVE food and you are without, then you are in scarcity and if you have guilt or negative emotions around food then it causes great pain. Try to find a neutral space with your relationship. If you can, sit with your list of emotions and begin to analyze them in detail. Give food the power during this exercise to tell you about your relationship. Who is the leader in the relationship –YOU or the food? Find out why you have difficulty with this aspect of life and then, if you choose, you can begin to move out of the dysfunction of food and into a life that is filled with experiences of which food is only one.

We leave you hungry for healing.
Namaste

FORGIVENESS

How willing are you to forgive? Or put another way, how forgiving are you? Does this topic make you feel tense or resistant? What feelings does it bring up for you? Do you feel that you are more often than not the "injured" party or the victim of the situation so why should you have to forgive?

What is forgiveness? It is simply the act of allowing something to be let go without strings, without condition and without expectation. Many of you say "I forgive you", but do you really? Is the memory erased? A common phrase is "I forgive, but I don't forget." Is that forgiveness or is it something pretty you tell your Self so that you can feel the superior one in the relationship? If you do not forget than have you forgiven? If you are holding on to the memory of the slight or hurt or problem, then it is still alive and real for you. It may be on the backburner of your mind, but that fire can flare at any time with little provocation.

Forgiveness says that if someone has transgressed you for some reason you choose to set it aside and move forward with your life. When you do not forgive you are stuck in the energy of the event. There is always a part of you that is harbouring anger or negativity that keeps you from living fully. The other person may have moved on, but there is a part of your Soul that is stuck in the event. If you leave enough pieces of your Soul in those places what energy do you have left for your life? There are many unthinking, cruel, stupid and unconscious beings sharing this planet with you, do you want to be one of them? Some cruelties are done deliberately; others are unconscious acts by unconscious people.

The important question is, where do you want to live? Do you want to live your life consciously, free of constraints from the past? If so, then begin today to make lists of things that you are still holding on to that are keeping you stuck. It doesn't matter if it is past relationships or current ones, begin the process now of honestly evaluating your relationship to these people. Where are you the problem? Where are they the cause of your concern? Then slowly begin the process of removing their control from your life, for ironically the longer and harder you hold on to being "right" about being "wronged" the longer you stay stuck in the past and unable to live in the now and enjoy the future.

We leave you in joy.
Namaste

CLARITY

Do you feel that you see life clearly and honestly or does it sometimes seem as though you are looking at it through a fuzzy lens? Does life seem to be a mumble jumble of thoughts and events and occurrences that tumble along with no seeming pattern or purpose? Do you feel confused or overwhelmed by the events of your life?

Clarity is an easily attainable position in life. It requires only that you put aside the daily mumble jumble of living, the "what if's" and the "could be's" and "might have been's" and see life is a simple path forward. Now a simple path does not mean an "easy" path or one that is not filled with detours and rough roads and even pitfalls, but it is a straight path forward even if it meanders.

Clarity comes when you take the time to sit with silence. The difficult part for most people is that you have so much chatter in your heads. Your lives are much filled with conversations and thoughts both external and internal. You may ask for the answers, but then you do not have the patience to wait for the questions to be answered. You want instant gratification rather than waiting for the answers to unfold. Fear is a big part of this process. Fear that the answers will not come or that they will not match what you hope and dream for and therefore while you may ask for the answers you also do not want to hear them.

Clarity is about simplicity. It is "less is more" in many ways. Let us say that you are currently experiencing some difficulty or troubling time. Do you sit quietly in meditation and gather strength from the silence and the healing provided or do you rush pall mall about talking about the problem, worrying over the problem and living with the problem? Your life continues to happen in a reasonably placid manner while this problem occupies some of your space. Do you pull your attention from the rest of life to feed the problem? Do you treat friends and family with anxiety and concern or do you attempt o put your concerns aside and be present in the moment with them. You might find great sustenance from the peace you find with other people not so intimately involved with your concerns for they have a perspective that is about life moving forward. Worry puts you back in the eddy of life. You stay stuck with the worry and upset.

Take a few moments today to think of something that is causing you upset. Take a few breaths and sit in the quiet. As your concerns come up to the surface allow them to bubble away, do not follow them, just allow. Try not to worry or get upset, just allow your Self these few minutes without chatter in your head. Then as you return from the quiet try to carry a piece of it with you or the "Peace" of it with you for the rest of the day, for the more you quiet your mind, the greater clarity you will receive. Your life is a beacon that is calling you forward. Look for the light, for the guidance and strength.

We leave peacefully.
Namaste

GUIDANCE

What do you seek when you ask for guidance?
Do you want the answers?
Are you seeking the last page of the book?
Do you want to know how it all ends?
Do you want the lottery numbers?
What does guidance mean to you?

We have used these extreme examples because there is much talk about wanting guidance but little understanding that each of you already received it. Most of you want someone outside of your Self to give you the answers. You use Tarot cards, I Ching coins, Ouiji boards, psychics, astrologers, mediums or some other method in the hopes that you will get very specific answers to your concerns fears and questions. You seem to trust the external more than the internal.

Why does someone outside of you validate the truth better than do you? First of all, it is not in your best interest for growth to want to know the outcome of future events. If it were, you would be given these gifts. Life is meant to unfold in the moment. It is meant to be lived with all the ups and downs, hills and valleys. What would become of you and your life if you were moving along the paths and enjoying every day and your job and your relationship only to have the sudden realization that in 10 years someone you love very much would have a lingering illness? Would you enjoy those ten years between the time of your current life and this life altering event? Would you live in joy and abandon or would you shut down and close your Self off for fear of this future event?

Life is meant to be lived each moment it occurs. It is a thrill ride in the truest sense, for you never know what is around the next corner or over the next hill. You can be in the bottom of despair today and tomorrow the ride of life could begin to rise meteorically upward and back to the heights of joy. Yes, it can also plummet from extreme joy to despair but what we are puzzled about is why you are all so resistant to the ride? If you have experienced first-hand or witnessed people going from the bottom to the top rapidly or from the top to bottom, why do you fear this? Have you not noticed that it is transitory? If you can go either way meteorically why does it frighten you when you are on the bottom waiting and why does it terrify you as the descent begins? Is there no memory or hope that it will rise up again?

Now if you are facing a decision and you would like to have guidance as to the best path to take, we recommend that you sit quietly and go within. Truly listen to your Self, not to all the noise, chatter and input from outside and not to all the noise, chatter and fear from within. Life is about choice. Some of you will make the choice easily and it will be the "right" choice. Others will find it more difficult and in hindsight it could appear to be the "wrong" choice, but we offer that all decisions bring you to the same place for your Soul's journey. The more you can release right/wrong and good/bad the happier you will be. If you sit in silence and meditation about that which you are troubled or want an answer, you will find the peace that will enable you to find the guidance you so desire.

We leave you quietly.
Namaste

SELF

Do you know who you truly are?

Are you well acquainted with your Self?

Do you know all the good/bad, positive/negative things about your Self?

Are you a friend to You?

Most of you do not want to discover who you are. You do not want to discover SELF. The fear is that you will come up short or lacking or be less than you imagined, but we find this fascinating because the reason you do not want to begin the journey is that you have already made up your minds that it is futile. You judge your Selves rather harshly. You find your Selves lacking in so many ways. You live with "shoulda, coulda, woulda's" about life events and your own personal courage. You are stopped by fear. You are stopped by anger. You are stopped by Self-esteem. You are stopped by the stories of your life – the ones you tell your Self and those that have been told to you. What fascinates us is your willingness to believe the stories you hear about your Self. Most of you are willing to believe the negative, judgmental, limiting stories. All the "can'ts" or all the reasons why not. Very few of you believe the uplifting or positive or empowering stories. Are you so conditioned to negativity that you cannot or do not want to hear the "good news?"

In the end all you have is YOU. Not even in the end. In every moment of every day there is one person and one person only upon whom you can depend. That is YOU. Your life may be blessed with a lot of love and support and family and friends, but at night when you sleep there is only you and perhaps your dreams. The only person you are guaranteed to know your whole life is YOU. Again, there may be others, but as far as a guarantee, YOU are it!

So think again about your relationship with this ONE person. Why do you want to spend your life in the company of someone you don't know, perhaps don't like and certainly don't respect? Interestingly, why do you constantly seek outside of your Self for "someone" to validate, love, support and care for you? Now that is not to say that these people won't appear in the form of parents, partners, lovers, and friends, but can you guarantee that they will ALWAYS be there? Why do you want this external validation and yet withhold the internal validation, the internal journey to Self-awareness and healing? What is so scary inside of you that you don't want to go in and find out?

If you could fix one thing about you today, what would it be? It does not have to be the "best" choice, just a choice of one thing you would like to improve or change. Sit with your choice for a few moments. How can you change this thing? What would be your first steps? How committed are you to seeing this change through? Can you commit today to focusing on this one thing – it is only ONE thing – to see the change into being? If you chose something "hard" that is your choice. If it seems too overwhelming or not possible, then pick another thing that is easier as your first attempt. Give your Self the commitment to begin the work to fix this ONE thing. Make a plan of action and follow it. Then, when it is complete look at your life and re-evaluate your efforts and how you feel now that this thing is complete. Then begin on all the rest.

We leave you in Self discovery.
Namaste

WORRY

How often do you worry about the smallest details of life?

Do you focus on all the “what ifs” and “could be’s?”

Do you obsess about the right and wrong of each thing that passes through your life?

How much time do you have in the day to worry through each aspect of life?

We would like you to take time this week noticing the number of times that you stop what you are doing to obsess about small details. Did you order the right thing to eat for lunch? Did you remember to turn off the iron or coffee pot? Did you write that letter correctly or should it have said this or left that out? Truly pay attention to the things that occupy your mind. In the greater scheme of things do they matter? Will the world end if any of these things are not handled correctly? Most of you spend your energy, brains, time and attention on things that do little to move your forward, if anything they keep you stuck or move you back. You allow your minds to focus on the minutia of life which keeps you out of the game of life. It seems that if all the “details” of your life can be made to be perfect then somehow you believe the rest of your life will work better as well.

Life is like a giant impressionist painting. It is made up of thousands of brush strokes of various colors, length, thickness and depth. If you stand up to close to the painting it appears to be just that - a lot of paint slapped onto a canvas, but as you slowly move backward from the canvas and you give it space, a beautiful portrait appears. Now if the brush strokes you are applying are small and controlled and worried and intense will the portrait have an open, alive airy feeling? If you allow the brush strokes of life to be applied mostly in long flowing strokes, trusting that the strokes will carry the message, you have a much greater chance of painting a masterpiece rather than a small study.

As you live your life in close quarters with your Self, always judging and worrying and rethinking; you shut down the possibilities of greater thoughts, more space and infinite possibility. For today we want you to just notice the worrying or rethinking that you do. Be honest with your Self; do not try to justify the worries as important or not important. Just notice them. If you can, write some down, if not maybe you can just have a piece of paper with hash marks on it that count the number of worries. As the week progresses begin to try to set the worriers aside and replace them with thoughts that uplift or empower. If this is too much, just set them aside for the moment and move forward with something else. Sometimes when you overwork the painting it turns to mush. Work on your masterpiece this week.

We leave in love and possibility.
Namaste

CHAOS

Life is still chaotic. You live in chaotic times with information occurring rapidly and constantly. There is no time to not know that something has happened because it is instantly transmitted. The transmission is one thing, but then it is instantly analyzed, judged, categorized, discussed and reviewed. All information is available to everyone all the time. Now this is not true of your personal information, but many of you have become sensitized to this way of living, so you feel raw much of the time. World catastrophes are instantly reported with pictures and interviews and judgments of who has not dealt with the situation "as it should be." How should it be?

Stop and think about this for a moment. When did you all become experts on the handling of every situation in the world? When did human suffering, natural disaster, every casualty of war become your business? There is much good that comes out of shining light in dark places, but there is also chaos. It becomes a part of your daily life to worry about people in a mudslide halfway around the world. You are all one and you are all connected, but why do YOU need to be focused on that event? All Souls have their own journey and each must experience it as the life they lead dictates. A tsunami hits in Sri Lanka and you worry about it in New York. A volcano erupts in the Pacific Ocean and it now must concern the people of Paris. The hue and cry that rises from the world community that YOU must help is immediate and many of you instantly go into action. Again, we say this is not all bad, but what is worrying to us is that all of this upheaval, this chaos if you will, is coming into your living rooms along with the normal chaos of living. There is very little way to insulate your Selves any longer and this begins to wreak havoc on your mental and physical Self.

How? You never shut down or rarely. Your compassion and caring is constantly being tapped for some remote part of the world or even your country. You are constantly bombarded with sad stories or sad events and this begins to make you feel that there is nothing good or safe or wonderful left in the world. It becomes increasingly difficult for you to feel "joy" or be "happy" in your life. What about all these suffering people? How can I be happy if they suffer?" The answer is that you can be happy. You are not suffering, they are suffering. If you can, send money that is wonderful, but then release the suffering and get back to your joy. If you cannot send money then send loving and gentle thoughts to them for strength and healing. That is enough, but then turn back to your own life and be joyful for your gifts and abundance. Be joyful that you are not in the tragedy, be joyful that you are alive and in good health and have shelter.

If you allow all the world events to constantly batter your tranquility you will be in chaos most of the time. In chaos there is no rest, there is no peace and it is difficult to create true happiness and joy. We need more joy-filled people to move out in to the world. In joy you are positive. In joy there is hope. In joy there is love.

We leave you filled with joy and possibility.
Namaste

BELIEVING

How willing are you to believe? We are not asking this from a position of wishing upon a star this time, we are asking from a place of willingness to believe negative or limiting things. Let us say that someone tells you something uplifting and complimentary. Do you believe them? Do you agree with this vision of your Self or do you immediately begin to give “evidence” of how they are wrong to believe or admire you? Now this stream of “proof” that they are wrong to believe in you or admire you, may be said out loud or be silent inside your head. The location doesn’t matter, what does matter is your response to compliments or more accurately observations about you as a person.

Let us say you are sailing along in life having a particularly good phase of life. Maybe in this time period you can forget about your limiting beliefs and you are truly just living life and it is working for you in ways it has never worked before. One day you come upon a person that is like a stone in the road or huge pothole in your life and they say or do something that stops you in your tracks. They might say something as simple as, “Are you really trained to do what you are doing?” Or they could say, “Who do you think you are being so happy or successful or whatever?” Does this person’s observation, judgment or belief knock you out of the bliss stream you are in? Do you allow an outside opinion to take from you the joy you are experiencing? If your answer is NO, then you are mastering the secret of life – go forward toward your dreams and goals with full out abandon and trust the outcome even without evidence of success. If, however, you do allow their statement or passing comment to knock you out of the stream of action, whose “fault” is that? Is it theirs for having an opinion? Is it yours for believing their opinion? Remember, the answer is always YOU.

What happens is that your Self-doubt, which might have been on hold or in abeyance or on vacation, comes hurtling back into your reality. It touches something within you that reminds you that you are not worthy, deserving or important enough to have what you want. It is Self-defeating behaviour because it should not matter to you what others tell you if you are in a pursuit of a dream. Think of the last negative thing that someone said to you, or that you perceived to be negative for it may not have been intended that way. What was actually said to you? Sit with it for a moment and truly think about what was said and then think about how you interpreted it. Can you see that you might have imbued the comment with more importance or meaning than was actually meant? What about the comment touched a belief inside of your Self that stopped you in your tracks? Where did that belief come from? If you can take a few moments to follow that back to the point or person in your life that caused the belief to be inserted into your psyche, then sit with that for a moment. Do you want to release that limiting belief? Would it be nice to let go of that critic or judge or negativity so that you could begin the forward journey again? Then lovingly do so. You can say something to the effect of:

“I release the belief that I am _____ and I forgive the person or event that caused me to hold onto that belief and most importantly I forgive my Self for ever having believed it could be true. Go in love.”

Try this for a while and you will begin to see that you can change what you believe from limiting to limitless.

We leave in limitless possibility for a future well lived.
Namaste

TENSION

How tense are you?

How tightly do you hold your Self?

Are your muscles relaxed and loose or
are your neck, shoulders and arms tight and stiff?

Observe your Self right now. Are you sitting calmly with ease or are you pulled up and tight? What are your thoughts like? Are you concerned about something or many things? Do you worry about the direction of your life, of other people's lives? Are you constantly on-guard and watching for mistakes, errors, missteps or falters? Do you expect the best to occur or the worst? Do you believe in others and their abilities to follow through or do the right thing? Do you trust that the world could continue to spin if you closed your eyes for a moment?

We know there are a lot of questions, but we truly want you to take the time to notice how many or few of those questions pertain to you and your way of living. Now the argument will be that it is your job or things will go awry if you let down your guard and that could be true. However we would like you to analyze if it is necessary for you to be so vigilant, so on guard all the time. When was the last time you truly relaxed? By this we do not mean laid down to rest or even just laid down to read or watch television, but really relaxed. Did you let all the worries and thoughts seep out of your mind and just go to a place of bliss and peace? When you are with friends are you calm and relaxed or is there always an edge to you?

Your society requires that many of you be constantly on watch. Due to the nature of communication, all mistakes, news, information is instantly transmitted and received. You are literally bombarded with data. The brain is a processor that runs your body and the more input the more it processes. Here's a secret however, if you put less into your brain and allow for more quiet and peace, the brain will begin to function at even higher levels than before. It will be able to take the data and work with it for a longer period of time. Think about how much you put into your brain in a ten minute period. Observe your Self for ten minutes. Notice the phone calls, interactions with co-workers or family, material that must be read and dealt with and then add in our favourite....all the instructions from within your head. The coaching, judging and criticizing that goes on within your own minds is phenomenal. Just listen actively for ten minutes one day and observe what you are processing in that short time, then begin to multiply that out into your daily existence.

Is it any wonder you are tense?

Begin to allow your Self five to ten minutes a day to just blank out your mind and be at peace. The tension will begin to flow out of you and you will begin to find bits of peace.

We leave quietly and in love.
Namaste

WORK

Do you work hard?

How much of your life is taken up with work?

What do you define as work?

Is work only where you get your paycheck?

Are you constantly working or do you avoid work at all costs?

What is work?

Work is really something to which you are dedicated. Now some of you react to that and think, “No, work is where I go each day to make a living,” but we want you to expand your visions and include all the effort you expend in a day. Stop and think of all the ways you use the word work in your life. Do you work on your Self? Do you work around the house? Truly think how you define work. Is it just effort? Is it always hard or challenging? Some of you go to the gym and work out. What we want you to do is spend a bit more time at your internal gym – working IN.

Again we come back to what you are willing to do for YOU. What is your willingness to go within and find out what blocks you have to joy, prosperity and love? If you look at this exercise just like an experience at a gym, you need to see all the phases of the experience. At the regular gym you have cardio-vascular, you have weight training and you have very specific machines or movements to build certain muscles or burn calories. Internally there are many ways to find SELF. There is meditation, there is the willingness to listen during these times of meditations for insight and guidance, there is the search for peace, the search for truth and the search for enlightenment.

Most importantly there is the search for YOU.

The YOU that is Spiritually fit.

The YOU that is alive in the complete quiet.

The YOU that wants to know how to overcome the upsets, frustrations and obstacles to happy living.

The answer is inside and YOU just have to be willing to work IN to find OUT.

We leave you in peace
Namaste

DARKNESS

How willing are you to let light into the darkness?

How available are you to understanding the magnificence of your being - that you are a child of God and therefore a reflection of His light and love?

Do you dwell in a world of possibility and hope or do you dwell in despair?

Are you more disheartened than enlivened?

Does life hold joy and excitement or is it something to be endured?

Life is a gift. It is a gift most of you don't cherish and most of you don't want to open it up all the way to truly see the gift. Some days the gift may not look as you thought it should, but that is where the magnificence of the gift truly lies – in the unknown – in the experiences that you are frightened of; in the challenges. It is how you ride out the bad storms of life that define who you truly are in this life and more importantly who you truly are in your Soul.

Can you be happy right here, right now? Can you be content with what you have today, in this moment? If you can, you have won most of the battle of life. It is easy to be happy and joyful and content when all the breaks are going your way, when life is as you picture it. It is when life is a bit stormier or darker or turbulent and you still maintain your balance that you find your true Self. Keep walking forward. Keep your head up. Keep a smile on your face. Find the laughter.

This is how you get to the end of a life with pride. It is in your dealings with the darkness and troubles that help define you. Triumph over adversity. Triumph over your own personal demons and you will be victorious in the end and you will have joy in the end and you will have Self.

We leave in light and love.
Namaste

PERSEVERENCE

How willing are you to persevere? In the face of no evidence, in the face of obstacles, difficulties, disappointment and detours, are you willing to continue toward the search for your Soul? The journey to Self is a long one that can be accomplished in the blink of an eye if you allow your Self to be vulnerable to Self.

What does that mean? There is the YOU that you believe is YOU. It is a person, character you have created that does this and says that and lives here and has these things and knows these people. That is the You, you are right now. How do you like YOU? Is that YOU happy, content, joyful, laughter-filled and content? Is that YOU at peace? If that is the case, then you have found Self, but if it is not content and joy-filled, then you simply have YOU.

Self is contented and at peace with what is – not with what should, could and will be. Self is awash in a sea of peace that says that storms may blow the sea and disasters can occur, but you know that Self will survive the bitter winds as well as the calm and beautiful seas. Contentment and surrender are the keys to this life of Self. There is no good in worrying about what might be or could have been for obviously it is not to be or it would have been. We realize that this is very convoluted talk, but yet it is not if you sit with it for a bit and allow it to be absorbed into you. It is what it is - Nothing more and nothing less. We have commented on this topic many times before, yet we return to it often because it is the biggest stumbling block for most of you.

Life does not match your pictures. Life is what is happening right here, right now. It is the shortage of money; it is the loss of a job or a loved one. It is a difficult job or a trying personal situation. It is more work than you had hoped it would be and it is less satisfying than you wish it were. It is life. It is a living, breathing thing that moves through the universe. Life has wars and death and births and accidents and starvation and cruelty and destruction. Life also has laughter, love, creation, beauty, salvation, redemption and possibility.

Limitless possibilities are awaiting each and every one of you as you move through this thing called life, but you have to want them. You have to want to put aside the depression, the sadness, the "poor me" or the negative Self-talk and strip your Self clean of it all and dive into life in your birthday suits….and begin to swim with abandon. Look at the opportunities that present themselves and notice how often you are a big NO to fun, to possibility, to opportunity. Often things do not look like opportunities, but they are just that; for you never know what is coming around the corner of life.

So, think about giving YOU up and begin the journey to Self. After all, most of you have probably bought books or listened to tapes about SELF AWARENESS why don't you try it rather than reading it or listening.

Jump into LIFE!!

We leave in love.
Namaste

AVOIDANCE

What do you avoid?

What do you sweep under the rug?

What do you hide from others about your Self?

When you sweep things that are necessary for your life under the rug, do you truly think they are no longer there, or do the dust bunnies of avoidance begin to rule your life?

Most people avoid that which they feel is too hard or too time consuming or too frightening or too insurmountable to deal with. They also avoid health issues, monetary woes and the cleaning up of relationships. Some people avoid confrontation, others avoid love. What do you avoid?

As you ignore or avoid things they begin to have larger meaning in your life. This seems in contrast to the whole point of avoidance. Yes, some things can fade into the background and simply disappear, but if you truly think about the things you are currently setting aside for "another time," are they disappearing? Avoidance is just the postponement of the inevitable. Now, some of you can argue that you have avoided something and "gotten away" with it. It has never raised its ugly head again. We would counter that it obviously has not "gone away" other wise you would not now be bringing it up as something you avoided. Sit with that for a moment.

The things in life that are irritants take up a lot of time. It is not necessarily time you pay much attention to or value as you do set appointments, but it is time you lose to the energy of avoidance. If you are avoiding a phone call or encounter with another person, do you have to screen your calls or have trepidation every time the telephone rings? Do you have to plan your day so that you don't "run into" this person? Do you give up social engagements because you do not want to see the person? How about business opportunities? If they are at your work place, are they keeping you from being the most efficient and effective you can be? Let us say it is a bill you cannot pay. Do you avoid calling the company or person to work out payment? Do you avoid the inevitable of the fact that you owe the debt and wait and worry about when they are going to come for payment? Do you have a medical condition that is troubling you? Do you not go to the doctor or postpone treatment because of what might happen? Then do you ever stop worrying about this condition, can you put it at rest?

The truth will set you free is a common statement. It is true. If you know what the situation is, you can make plans to deal with it, but if you avoid it you are so busy making plans on how to avoid it, you do not ever resolve it on your terms. This is what is important - Resolution on your terms. They may not be the answers and outcomes you most desire, but the handling of the situation becomes yours to control. You choose how you want it to happen. Others may dictate the terms of how it will play out, if it is a debt or a medical condition or even the settling of an upset between people, but if you initiate the resolution it gives you an advantage because you have chosen resolution rather than avoidance.

Begin resolving life so that you can fully live each day in joy and abundance of Spirit.

We go in joy.
Namaste

FOCUS

Focus on the point between your eyebrows and slightly above them, for this is your Third Eye. This is a place that allows you to focus your attention, energy and Self. It is a place that if you concentrate enough upon it, it will allow you to travel to kingdoms of bliss, enlightenment and joy.

It is an easy thing to do, to put your attention on this spot and just "allow" it to remain there. Breathe deeply and rhythmically, allowing the breath to calm you, lull you into a peaceful, loving place. Focus.

Many of you talk about not being able to focus. You are too scattered, too frenetic, too busy running from place to place with no purpose, except you think there is a purpose to your frenetic activity. What if it were as simple as moving your eyes upward and placing them in the position of gazing into the Third Eye? What if you could take your Self out of the craziness of life for a few moments and just focus the attention and energy on this spot.

Try it. Think about something that has been troubling you or causing you to feel out of balance. Take a few deep breaths and move your eyes to the Third Eye. Then just breathe. Allow any thoughts that come bounding in trying to intrude to move through. Do not keep them, just excuse them and send them on their way. Just breathe and focus on this spot. Allow for peace. Allow for calm. Just breathe.

Practice this several times a day. Use it when you are feeling stressed, out of sorts, alone, frightened or angry. Just allow for the time, maybe two to five minutes. The key is to allow, let and give your Self the permission to just breathe and rest in the calm of the third eye.

We leave you focused and in sight.
Namaste

PERFECTION

What if getting over your upsets, problems and distortions were just as easy as unzipping a jacket or coat? What if you could imagine that you could simply focus and then unzip the cloak of distortion that you wear? Would you do it? How willing are you to give up your problems, your cares, your distortions and your faults? We are talking about those things that you carry around with you and despair about constantly.

Let us take money problems. What if you could sit in meditation and see all of your money issues congealed upon you as if a giant suit of debt and worry? As you look at this suit and the weight of the worry and turmoil, you would begin to love it as it is. You would begin to see that it is a burden that you have created through mismanagement and scarcity, forces out of your control or whatever has occurred to create this debt. Now as you look at this giant suit you are wearing you begin to meditate on a different reality, you begin to look underneath the suit at the true essence of your Self. You begin to notice that you are not these mistakes or profligate spending, but rather you are a person of integrity that for whatever reason was unconscious about money for a while and have reached this place. Now, if you meditate on the transformation of the behaviours that brought you to this place, you begin to realize that you could allow the true essence of your Self to shine through and remove this distortion of improper money management. By concentrating and realizing who you truly are with money, you could begin to strip away this burden of debt or mismanagement. How willing would you be to remove this suit of debt? To simply unzip it and move out of it; never to return? Most of you would say .... "Yes, I want the miracle of just unzipping and walking away."

Here is the real test; however, how willing would you be to do it knowing that your ways of spending could never return to what they had been? Your management of money from this place forward would be in complete alignment with what you earn or receive each month. No more credit card debt, no more borrowing to have something today rather than save for it tomorrow? Perhaps no more new cars that are only leased and never purchased or new electronic toys or clothes that fill a closet and rarely are worn or jewelry or whatever it is that consumes your money. Maybe you would stop going to restaurants to eat and only would eat at home, where it is less expensive. Think about how your life would be different if you lived within your budget. Can you honestly say that you are willing to live in alignment with the money in your life in exchange for removing this cloak of debt?

The point of this lesson is that most of you are unhappy with some aspect of your life. It may be money, it may be weight or body image or it may be relationship. It could be health. The question in it all, if you could have the perfection you seek, are you willing to live the life required to have what you want? Or to put it another way, are you willing to live in alignment with your dreams so that you may have them?

We leave you contemplating this.
Namaste

IRRITATION

How much time do you spend each day being irritated about something or many things?

What causes irritation?

Is it the lack of control, judgment, fear, anger or just plain annoyance?

Why do you allow things to annoy or upset you?

Even if something seems out of your control, it is in your control how you react to it. Is that statement in and of itself irritating?

You are the only one in control of your emotions and reactions. You are the master of that and since you all love control so much, we would think that you would want to control your emotions better. Why better? We notice that you allow many others to intervene in your wonderful life and "ruin" it or upset it or cause you distress. Why do you allow it to happen? People are just people. Some of them are kind, efficient, smart and helpful. Some are lazy, stupid, inefficient, not good listeners and wasteful. Some are hateful, mean, conspiratorial, judgmental and petty. Some are just there. Their behaviours are not actually meant to annoy or upset you; they are just busy being the human being they know how to be.

Now some of you are shocked about the fact that another person would want to be "that way," but they don't know that they are "that way," they just are. Yes, some people go out of their way to be unpleasant and they think life is all about them, but then don't you? If you are being irritated by their belief that life is “all about them” then don’t you think that you are thinking life should be all about you? We can hear the cries of how Selfless and giving you are, how often you “let it go” and get on with your life, but do you? Do you just watch these other people struggling though their day and bless them and move on or do you watch them and then call your friends or co-workers and have a nice gabfest about their inappropriate behaviour, their obtuse behavior or whatever you deem it to be? Do you carry it around and sigh and think about how annoying or inappropriate they are? Do you have a running dialogue about the drivers on the road? Do you talk about the problems you have with friends or spouses? Now some of it is cathartic and helps you move through things you do not understand, but the bottom line is most people are not trying to be irritants; they are simply trying to get through the day, just as you are attempting to live your life. Understand that we are not condoning ugly behaviour, we think the world would be a much happier place with people who meditate and try to live on a Spiritual level, but we are not irritated that this is not so. We simply keep trying to find those that will listen and begin to see that there is another way to live.

So, the next time you are irritated, remember that there is another way to be at peace and in joy. Control your Self and then see what you can affect in the world.

We leave in love.
Namaste

BLISS

Have you ever experienced pure bliss?

Have you just been in the moment with nothing in the way and pure love, light and peace at your disposal?

There is no noise, no upset, no distresses, no judgments, just nothing. It is the place of total calm and peace. It is the place of everything and nothing. It is joy. There is nothing against which you can push. It is the place of true creation. It is a place of true Spirituality, for you have left behind your needs, wants, desires and imperfections and elected to float freely in the place of infinite joy.

How do you find this place? You practice going within and putting aside your agenda and your thoughts and your need to control and you just float in nothingness. There are no answers in bliss and yet everything is contained therein. There is complete silence and yet it is the most wonderful "sound" you will ever hear.

There are no sensations, but you sense them all. It is a place of complete rejuvenation. It is the ultimate spa day. All of your needs are taken care of and yet nothing is happening. What could be better?

We would like each of you to try to find this place at least once. It is all well and good to struggle and strive for messages and insights as you meditate, but it is best to finally reach the point on any given day in which nothing happens and it is the best thing that ever happened.

Continue to strive to the goal of bliss – of nothing so that you can have everything.

We leave peacefully and blissfully.
Namaste

IMPORTANCE

What is important? What matters to you, to society, to the world? Many of you think that you have a world view, that you are focused on what is best for mankind. This is very altruistic and kind, but do you know what is important to you? What is truly important?

What do you need, want, desire? In the final analysis what things do you truly need to keep in your life and what could you live without? What matters? Is it health, wealth, fame, family, love, lust? Take some time to think about where your life is going and what you are doing with this thing called life.

Is the direction the one you want? Think about the balance in your life. Is there balance? If you have too much in any one pot or place it causes imbalance and then you feel out of sorts, tired and unwell. Draw a picture of your life. Put all the baskets or aspects of your life down on a piece of paper – work, play, family, school, friends, charity work, Spirituality, whatever you can think of that you do in your life or that you "should" do or would like to do or have. Next assign percentages to each basket of life, then draw them based on size. Look at the picture. It will tell you how you are out of balance with things in your life. It will tell you why you feel off or unbalanced or unhappy or unwell. Just like with food, it is the blend of things that you put into your body that makes you feel well – it is the blend of activities in life that give you psychic wellness. If you work too much or too little you are off, if you play too much or too little you are off, if you are alone too much or never alone you are off. It is about the extremes of life.

Think about the last time you felt rested or at peace. What was going on in your life, what were you doing? Think about how you feel right now as you read this and then again, look at the drawing. Finding the balance will help you to understand where the holes are, where the fix can come from. You will find out what is important. You have all the answers, but you need to understand where they are and what to do with them.

We leave you in peace and balance.
Namaste

WAITING

What are you waiting for?
Do you have the sense you are waiting?
What do you want that you are sitting abeyance about?

Life often happens for most of you, tomorrow or in the future. When this or that happens THEN you will do what you want or you will travel or move or change jobs or visit friends. Life is happening right here and right now. It may happen in the future but the only thing you can be certain of is right here and right now. What do you get out of postponing the things you want to do or wish you could do? Now in some ways this may seem at odds with what most people tell you about postponing your enjoyments until you can afford them or have time or your children are grown, but are they mutually exclusive? So, we ask you to sit and think about something you are postponing or waiting for and determine what is keeping you from having this “thing.” Are you waiting for someone to change their attitude or way of being? Are you waiting for some magic occurrence that will make everything all right? The longer you wait, the more your life is on pause. Do you have an optimistic view of life or a fatalistic view? Do you believe that if you keep doing what you are doing, that things will work out? How do you see the world?

Life is occurring as you read this. It is running by you and forward into some unknown and you might want it to be static. Think about people who have just been given a medical diagnosis that might be life ending or certainly life-altering. What happens to those people? Some just give up, some “fight” which we find interesting because what are they fighting and some wake up and realize that this thing called life is a precious commodity that most of you waste daily. This is it for now, this thing called life and most of you are asleep and unaware that great things are happening every day.

So, we ask that you look at your focus and your mind set and the time you spend each day of this life worrying, waiting and being upset or angry or sad. Stop waiting, stop wasting, stop wishing that it were different and dive in and begin to do all those things that you "wish" you had right now. Begin to live and stop the wait. Think of it like the restaurants that give you the buzzer to let you know when it is your turn to sit down – the page of life is calling and it is your turn. Stand up, go in and get going.

We leave at full throttle.
Namaste

TECHNOLOGY

What is it? You all live in a very technical age. Is it your computers, I-Pods, cell phones, PDA'S, Wi-Fi and all the other bells and whistles that you believe are required to live life in the 21st century? What about the technology of living?

The machines and accessories only facilitate things. They may speed up communication or make it more accessible than it previously was to the majority of people, but what are your life skills? What is the "technology" that you need to run your daily life? Are you happy with all these machines? Do they make your life fuller and happier and more joyful? In many cases we think that they make your lives more burdened and less free to explore the Spirituality of living.

So it is Spiritual technology that we want to talk about today. How willing are you to invest in that technology? Is it a "must have" in your life? Meditation and the journey within bring you untold rewards and gifts. It answers many of life's questions. It provides solace and comfort. It enlivens and invigorates you and your body. The journey to Self is a fantastic voyage into the constant unknown, but it is one without fear, without anger, without judgment. It is a journey to the center of your being. It is the journey to the void, which is bliss, which is nothing and everything and yet you do not want to take the time to learn the steps to reach this magnificent place. You will spend hours with earplugs in your ears listening to the latest music. You will sit for hours playing computer games or checking Emails or surfing the web, but you don't seem to be able to take five, ten and maybe even twenty minutes a day to invest in You and more importantly your Soul or Self.

What is your Soul's journey? Maybe you will never know even if you meditate, but we can guarantee that your Soul will be more free, more peaceful and more enlightened when you take the time to allow for the calm and peace it needs. Take a quick inventory of everything you do during the day. Look at the time you MUST set aside for work, for the gym, for errands, for eating, for drinking or for whatever you use to fill your time. Can you not find that five or ten minutes per day to sit quietly and breathe your way to freedom?

The technology for this is very old and maybe you think it is antiquated and are waiting for it to come out on a computer or video game or on a DVD or a CD or that you will be able to download it from somewhere to your MP3, but it is not of this time. It is of a time when all that was required was YOU. Just you as you are in the moment to take the time to breathe, relax and journey to galaxies unknown. We hope you can find your way to our technology for it, in the end, is your salvation.

We leave in contemplation.
Namaste

WAITING

Are you waiting for the BIG revelation?
Are you waiting for guidance?
Are you waiting for direction?
Are you waiting for purpose?

It may be a long wait. These things are not always given in the format depicted in Spiritual and Biblical and religious texts. Yes, if you consistently meditate and allow your Self to become devoid of thought, illumination can appear, but how many of you are able to be devoid of any thoughts? This is not a judgment or condemnation, but rather a statement of truths. Much of life comes in the action of it. Most of the things you seek are in action, not in repose. Let us explain.

If you are stuck wondering what to do, where to go, how to live, then you are in an emotional eddy of sorts. You are confused and longing for something and trying to hear or learn or create from a place of unrest, unhappiness or confusion. This is very difficult because rather than listening or attuning to your guidance, you are running around in your heads wondering what is best or right or grand enough for you to waste your time on. Since you can't hear the answers in the cacophony of thoughts or feel an answer in a state of paralysis; you just sit and wait some more. If you choose one thing, just one thing that sounds like it might possibly, maybe be on the road to where you want to go; and begin to put energy into it and life and happiness and joy, things will begin to happen. Action needs energy and energy needs action. They are symbiotic. Begin to move. Join a group or begin to talk happily and excitedly about whatever this one thing is so that you can begin to give it life and breath and hope.

As you begin to move down the experience of this one thing you will begin to notice that you were not so alone, as you believe. You will begin to get more energy and excitement in your life and you will begin to feel alive again or maybe for the first time. The universe will begin to align with your energies in an action-oriented, positive way, just as they have been aligning for you in a tired, passive, hopeless way. That is all you have to do with this exercise. .... PUT ONE THING into action. Make a phone call, tell someone your idea or vision or just talk about the future and its possibilities. Be in joy.

We leave you in action and joy.
Namaste

CARE

Do you care for your Self?

Do you treat your Self with love, admiration, gentleness and care?

Do you dote on your Self?

Do you cater to your every whim?

Do you treat your Self as you would your loved ones, your partner, spouse, children or even pets?

How much CARE do you give to YOU?

Now we are not asking how many treats you give your Self or indulgences such as things or food or whatever you use to deaden your senses or give your Self momentary joy. What we want you think about is the time, attention and value you proffer to your Self. Do you take care of your body? Are you mindful of its needs, aches, pains, or workings? Do you eat the right things and avoid excess in sugars, alcohol and caffeine? Do you eat a balance, healthful diet that energizes you and allows for the maximum energy or do you overeat or under eat or eat on the fly as you are doing everything else? Do you exercise or move in a way that is energizing or again is it out of balance with too much or too little? Do you listen to your body; we mean truly listen and then do what is asked?

It is time to attune your Self to what you need. Now many lament that they cannot "hear" the messages given, but we would refute that claim. If your body is hurting in some way or you are not sleeping or you feel out of sorts, you are "hearing" that you are not taking care of your Self. Do you listen? How many of you have allergies to things you eat or breathe? Do you avoid those things or do you medicate to be able to live with them? Is the food you don't process well that important that you must eat it and then have your body be out of alignment? With airborne allergies, do you know what is truly causing them? Perhaps you could be allergic to foods you are ingesting and that could be exacerbating the airborne allergies. You might just be out of balance but how would you know?

So many of you want to be at peace and at a place of calm where you can meditate and be enlightened, but you are wanting to do this from a place of dis-ease or discomfort. When your body hurts or is out of alignment it takes your attention away from the inner peace that is yours. The journey to Self is harder when you have to overcome all the other things before you can sit peacefully and quietly. If you have too much stress or anxiety, how easy is it going to be to sit quietly for five or ten or more minutes? If you ache can you sit quietly and just be at peace and meditation. Think about it. Your bodies do an amazing job for you and yet you abuse them and then lament your lack of focus or peace.

Begin this week to take care of your Self. Listen to your body. Listen to the clues and the hints and the roadmap to wellness and begin to walk down that path. The joy that will be available as you leave the weights of unhealthy living and take on the mantle of health will move you astronomically forward in your journey.

We leave with great hope and love.
Namaste

ANXIETY

Are you anxious about something?

Dreading the future or anxiously awaiting something that you sense or know is about to happen?

Do you have no feelings or emotions about the future?

What we are asking is where are you living right now?

Are you living in hope and possibility?

Are you living in fear and dread?

Are you living in "is that all there is?"

What is your excitement level about life?

What is robbing you of joy?

What is keeping you from realizing your dreams or hopes?

Sit for a few minutes and analyze your mood or state of mind. Really sit quietly with YOU and feel into how you are truly being right now with your life. Can you list the things that are causing you to feel as you do? By this we mean that whatever the emotion is, can you put into thoughts and words why you are experiencing the emotion? So, if you are happy or joyful or hopeful; what is causing you to feel that way right now? The question is the same for anxiety, sadness, despair or depression. If you are in a neutral space, then what is causing this place of quiet and nothing? If you take the time to be quiet with your Self, then you can perhaps begin to glimpse the reasons for your moods and then you can begin to make changes if you so desire.

Many of you have feelings of upset and anxiety and yet you do not know the true source of the upset, you only know the feelings or sensations. You cannot begin to change anything about your Self until you are aware of what is the root of the problem and maybe not even the root but the major branch leading back to the root. One belief system can have many branches that are created as new situations crop up regarding the fear or belief system. The most perfect thing would be if you could immediately identify the root because then you could begin to deal with the issue at its source, but even finding a main branch and effecting a change there can work wonders on moving you off of this place of fear and into possibility or at least peace.

Please work with this for as long as it takes to find the deeper meanings or feelings you are having and then you can begin to lessen the anxiety and fear and worry and move more joyously into the mainstream of life.

We leave in great hope.
Namaste

FAITH

How much faith do you have in your dreams? Please note that we did not say "wishes," for as we have written before there are vast differences between dreams and wishes. Dreams have form and substance that allow them to be called into being; they are more akin to desires. If you desire and dream you begin to put energy out into the world that will allow those things to become more real and concrete.

So now back to dreams and your willingness to put energy into the creation of that which you want. As you begin to analyze your life, one of the things that is important to be clear about is what you want and where you desire to go on this ride called life. What is it you truly desire? Some would say you must be very specific but some times you are too specific. You want only this one person or one job or one house or one something. That is rather limiting because maybe those things are not in your best interest or part of your destiny or karma. The important thing to remember, however, is that the essence of those things may very well be a part of your life, so being less specific can be helpful.

Write a general plan of what you would like your life to look like. Where would you like to work? What type of job? Make the description delicious and exciting and full of life. You do not have to name the company or position, but rather what would you like to be doing to enliven your life. The work might have nothing to do with a corporation or a traditional job, so do not think that this is limiting. Describe your day and what you do and how you feel as you are doing it. Make it come alive. Now do this with each thing in your dream. Describe the friends, family and partners that inhabit this world, the location or weather that you live in and how you are feeling and acting and being in this picture. Then set it aside and get about living. From time to time you can review your life story and maybe make changes. Begin to behave “as if” you already have these things you desire. Be joyful where you are right now, knowing that this world that you have created and are calling forth can be yours. Then have the faith to know that as you move seamlessly and joyfully through everyday living, small changes are beginning to occur. Do not despair if they are not immediate and do not look for “signs” at every moment. Just put it into play and live. After a few months we ask that you look at your story and at your current life. See where they might be matching up. Now many of you dream, so sometimes the symbols are hard to decipher, but allow for simple things such as an energy shift or a perception shift to occur. The key to anything you want in this life or any is to set your intention, make it come alive through visualization and writing and then let go of the outcome and live as joyously as you can with FAITH that all things will be as they should be.

We leave you in love.
Namaste

WORRY

What if you were to give up worry and just allow? What if rather than worrying you calmly asked for what you need, the best outcome or help and then set that thing aside and waited for the outcome? What would your life look like then? Most of you spend a lot of time, energy, and expense on worry. You think about what you can do and how you can do it and who should do what and how you want others to act rather than sending out a simple request.

"Lord, let me please see the answer to ____."

That is all that is really needed.

"Please let me see the answer to ______."

We say it again because it is a very simple, yet powerful request. The art of using it is the art of letting go of the outcome. Ah, there is the problem. Are you willing to let go of the outcome? Do you truly know what is best for you or planned for you or awaiting you? Sometimes what awaits is better than you can ever imagine and other times it may be a difficult outcome, but in the end how does the outcome move your life forward onto a different direction or path?

There are many defining moments in life where a decision, choice or situation beyond your control completely changes the course of your life. Do you sit and do "shoulda, coulda, wouldas" about it and wish for something else or do you get it instantly that this has changed the scenery of your life and you need to wake up and begin down this new path. It is a chance for exploration and creativity and a whole new perspective and yet most of you want to run back and cling to what was, even if what was did not "make you happy" or was not easy or pretty or right for you. Each life altering event gives you a fantastic opportunity to go in a direction to explore this thing called life. Why are you so afraid of the future? Why are you so afraid of the unknown? There are no monsters waiting, there is only your Soul's journey and if you listen closely and you push aside the human quality of fear, there is a magnificent ride called life and living and hope and adventure awaiting you.

The famous quote "The only thing you have to fear, is fear it Self" is true beyond measure. You are never ALONE in this journey; we are always with you and you must trust that even when the road is dark or completely obscured, there are those of us waiting to help you along the path. Take the help and leave the worry. Take the proffered hands that reach out to you and get moving.

Don't Worry – Be Happy.

We leave in peace and enormous love.
Namaste

CALM

How calm are you?

How placid is your daily life?

Do you allow for quiet and peace during the day
or is it constant chatter and thoughts and
deadlines and negative thoughts?

How calm are you?

To answer this question, imagine a placid lake with a smooth, glass-like surface with no ripples or bumps to disturb it. Is that what you life looks like? We would answer NO for most of you, for even though you may be living a life of peace and calm there will always be small ripples. Look, however at the surface of your lake. What does it look like? Are there small storms occurring all round it? Are there waves on your lake's surface? How about swirling eddies of confusion or emotion or anger or upset? If you were to describe your lake to someone what would be the words you use?

What would it feel like to be just calm? No upsets, no worries, no control, just the state of floating quietly along? Does that appeal to you or does it seem too boring or too easy or too frightening? Imagine your Self floating for a bit, just calming and feeling the emotions that arise. If it seems as though it would be a welcome relief, then try to just lie quietly and breathe in and out in long slow breathes and relax your Self into the picture of calm. Allow your Self to just float or lie in complete calm for five or ten or more minutes. As any worrying thoughts come up or things disturbing to the calm, just gently push them away and float calmly over to another part of the lake. Allow the peace and quiet to integrate into your being. Breathe in the calm; breathe in the nothingness of this experience. Do not judge or fret or try to control the experience, just be in it floating and worry free.

When you return from your calming voyage on the lake of life, how do you feel? Is it someplace you would like to go again? Is it something that you would like to use when things are feeling a bit out of control or jangled? If so, use this as a form of meditation and rest. Allow your Self the quiet gift of calm and peace.

We leave you in peace.
Namaste

THOUGHTS

What thoughts do you think?

What runs through your mind?

Is it positive and uplifting or is it negative and foreboding?

Are your thoughts motivating or do they keep you stuck?

How quiet is your head?

Thoughts have more power than you can imagine. They are ideas, if you will, that float unbidden through your consciousness. You could see them like a great freeway of cars whizzing by. Do you notice all the cars? Do you notice only the pretty ones that you would like to own or admire? Do you curse the other drivers or judge the car they are driving? Are you constantly in rush hour or do you drive freely and effortless along the highway of thoughts? Are you worried or frustrated by the conditions of the highway?

You may think this a frivolous analogy, but take a moment to think about how you are as you drive along the roads in reality? Are you a tense driver or does it seem effortless? Are you observant of the other cars or the scenery or are you on your phone constantly trying to be in two places at once? Now transfer that analysis into your mind. Do you attach to uplifting and empowering thoughts or do you focus on what is wrong? Do you allow bad thoughts/drivers to pass you and get out of your way or do you pursue them to prove something to them? Do you politely allow good thoughts to get in front of you or do you try to cut them off? How observant are you of your own thoughts. Do you try to avoid those thoughts that do not serve you or are not in your best interest?

Thoughts have power. You can say whatever you want out loud to others and hope they believe you, but if what you are saying in your thoughts to your Self constantly is what you truly believe it will be very difficult, if not impossible, to manifest that which you say you desire. If you think of your thoughts as your desires how would that make you feel? Or to put another point on it, if you realized that all the negative things you say about your Self, your family, your loved ones and humanity are truly what you believe, what will your world look like?

If your life is not as you want it to be right now, could it be that you are not careful with your thoughts? Saying what you do not want is as powerful as saying what you do. If you state an affirmation daily that is uplifting and positive and then you allow your thoughts to poison you with negativity all day, you are going to be “surprised” that your affirmation is not working. You must move the giant ship of thoughts in the right direction. You must begin to become more aware of that which you think and stop your Self from the harmful and negative qualities.

Be conscious of all the things that move through you daily. Every time you think an unkind thing about your Self or someone else, cancel that thought and put something more positive or at least neutral in its place. You will find that this will begin to move you to a life that is happier, more joyful and working as you wish it would.

We leave you along the highway of life, driving in sunlight and joy.

Namaste

POTENTIAL

You all have potential. For what, is what many of you wonder? Perhaps you heard that too much growing up and it is a word that has a lot of charge for you. You have great potential. You are not working up to your potential. Potential is simply that you could be or do anything.

Potential is just the promise of something as yet unrealized. It means that within you right now there are untapped reservoirs of strength, courage, energy or creativity. Why does it remain untapped or in waiting? Are you too worried that you "don't have what it takes?" Is it too much trouble? Do you not desire the things that you have believed are awaiting you? Potential is not a negative word, it is not a condemning word, but you allow it to be that in thinking that if you have potential you are obviously not working hard enough or fast enough or smart enough.

Let us look at it as an untapped natural resource. Think about a time in you life where you were called upon in a situation to do something that you thought not possible or overwhelming or frightening, but in that moment or moments you had no choice but to push through your fears and perform the action. All you did was to call forth reserves of your personal power to push you through the situation. If those reserves of power can be called forth in crisis, can they not be called forth in quiet and calm? Do you need to be in chaos to call forward your best Self? Are you that indolent? We do not believe that needs to be the case, but what does need to shift is the belief system that you do not have the resources you need right here, right now.

Most of life is about pushing the boundaries of safety. It is about taking those leaps of faith with no evidence. It is about trying the unknown and understanding that while it might seem scary from where you are standing, it truly is an illusion. The walls you create in your lives are truly invisible fortresses you build about your Selves to keep you “safe.”

What is “safe?” SAFE is a prison you build for your Self to keep the world away. You believe that you are keeping out hurt or harm or unnecessary activities or people. The “safer” you become, the more isolated you are in life. There is no “safe” but there is living. Living is full of noise and upsets and chaos and laughter and tears and love and anger and ups and downs. It is a roller coaster ride as we have said many times. It is full of exhilarations and swooping twists and turns. It is your choice to let the wind hit your face and laugh in the face of the unexpected turns and swoops or to cower under the seat and hope it goes away soon. Grab on to life and embrace the ride. LIVE fully and passionately each day and know that you are “safe” in God’s love and in this journey called life.

We leave laughing all the way.
Namaste

JEALOUSY

Are you jealous of something or someone?
What causes the jealousy?
What do they have that you do not?
Why can you not have what they have?
Why do you want what they have?

Jealousy is driven by scarcity. It is a small way of seeing and experiencing the world. It is an expression of lack and also a very Self-defeatist sort of approach to living.

To look at another and envy or covet what they have is another way of saying that your life is not of importance or meaning. When you covet what others have you are not living in your life, in your Soul's journey or in the moment. You came here to live YOUR life. You are in control of YOUR life.

What are you doing with it? What do you wish were different? Do you wish for more money, greater beauty, a partner, a child, a car, a house or a job? What do you wish for that you do not have? What does it matter what someone else possesses? That is their life. If you are not happy in your life, how willing are you to work for the things you desire? Do you think they are unattainable for you? If they are, how does it ruin your life to not have them? Take an inventory of the things that cause you envy or jealousy. Be very honest with the list.

Now, sit and analyze the list. How many of the things seem a bit frivolous when they are put on a list? How many truly matter? Of those things that truly matter, are any of them attainable? Please do not decide they are not attainable because of limiting belief, but rather that they might not be physically or emotionally attainable. If you are 6 feet tall and wish to be 5 foot 2 inches that is not reasonable. If you wish to change things dramatically in your physical being there is only so much you can accomplish in life, but there are some things that might make a difference through exercise or better nutrition or overall care of your body. Read the list again, what do you long for or believe you need to have a happy life? Are the needs mostly external? If so, how will they make you happier or more compassionate or loving or complete?

Life is about living. It is about connecting with other humans and it is most importantly about your Soul's journey. Begin to listen more to your Soul and not so much to your external needs or trappings. It is an interesting fact that as you begin the journey to your Soul, many external things begin to change as a result. It is a restoration from the inside out and it is the one that lasts.

Be in joy and in love and in peace.
Namaste

ALLOWING

What do you "allow" into your life?

Do you allow for abundance, for miracles, for events unforeseen or imagined?

Do you allow the unknown?

Do you allow possibility?

Do you believe that if you can leave enough space in your life to allow for things unknown and unseen that they will occur?

Most of you allow very little into your lives. You want to control the outcomes and so, therefore you have guards at the gate of living that keep you small and afraid and alone. You want life to look a certain way and contain only certain people and certain jobs. You believe that life is supposed to be one way and one way only and that is YOUR WAY. What if there were another way? One that is filled with excitement and expectation of surprise rather than expectation – PERIOD!!? What would living look like then?

Many of you shut down possibility because to you it is the unknown, to you it is unplanned, to you it is out of control. We have talked about control many times before, but it bears repeating. You control nothing really. Life is a madcap ride through experiences. They are just experiences with really no charge to them until you begin to label them as good/bad, abundant/scarce, happy/sad, fun/scary or whatever you choose in that moment to allow them to be. What if they were just experiences that allowed you the full spectrum of emotions? What would that feel like?

Life is just an opportunity to have the full spectrum of emotions. Some of the time you will laugh and some you will cry. Some of the days will be easy and bright and full of fellowship and sunshine. Some of the days will be harder, more challenging, darker and more difficult. The thing to remember is that life is a continuum of movement. If you put your arms to your side and float through life you have a much better chance of enjoying the ride along the way. There will be less resistance and therefore less tumult. Being at peace with "what is" allows you to live each moment fully. Being present in each moment brings you riches beyond measure because if you can be present in each moment you are TRULY ALIVE.

Go out today and live in the moment, experience the sensations of living and embrace the joyous thing called LIFE!

We leave you alive.
Namaste

RELEASE

What are you willing to release? To answer this you have to know what you are holding on to and why. Perhaps the "why" is not as important as the identification of the "what," but it is of use to you to know both things. Many of you give lip service to wanting things in your life to be different. You would like a better job, or partner. You would like a better body or health. You desire to have less stress and more abundance. Some of you may believe that you are working on the things you are hanging onto, but yet they do not change. What is in the way? What needs to be released?

Take a stressful situation in your life. What about it do you want to transform? What is the root of the stress or upset? What part of the situation is within your control? As you know from other meditations, not much is in your control other than your conscious and unconscious decision of how to react to life situations. So, given that, what do you control in this situation? The less you try to control the outcome, the more free you are to release any negative or controlling thoughts or beliefs. If you are unhappy with your co-workers and find they are not as efficient or directed as you believe they should be, are you willing to release your perceived control over their actions? If you are the manager of this group, are you willing to allow each to perform their tasks and then objectively evaluate their performance? If you are, then you can release a lot of the control or micro-managing that you are doing. If you are in a situation where someone higher up than you is not doing their job, can you put in better boundaries to your responsibility and allow them to succeed or fail on their own merits?

Releasing is an art. It is about being able to see where you are holding too tightly to the reins of a situation in the hopes of directing or controlling and instead you are creating more stress, worry and work.

If you are angry with someone, can you release your anger? We are not saying that you are wrong and they are right when you are feeling so righteous about your position. What we are saying is that if you can release your anger toward them, you lift a burden from your Self that opens your life up more fully. In the end, it is your life that matters and the only one in control of your life is guess who, YOU!

Releasing limiting, negative and controlling beliefs will work wonders toward getting you more energy, better health and more laughter. You will appear to be younger, happier and healthier to those around you without a spa treatment or face-lift or diet. You will lighten your load and therefore it will begin to reflect in your entire being. The more you release, the lighter you become. Take time today to look in all the storage places of your life and begin to release and let go of limiting and negative beliefs that are keeping you stuck and unhappy and small.

We leave you living large.
Namaste

CAMOUFLAGE

Who are you really?

Do you know your Self intimately?

Do you know all your fears, worries and upsets?

Do you know what stops you from having what you want?

Again, who are you really?

Many of you camouflage your Self. You put behaviours, addictions, upsets and worries in place of who you truly are and then you feel unhappy or empty or lonely. This makes perfect sense because if you keep hiding your true Self, you will feel unfulfilled. So again, who are you? Make a list of your qualities, all of them whether you would view them as good or bad or strong or weak. Are you kind, sympathetic, judgmental, withholding, joyful, reserved? Write a description of your Self. Then as you look at this list begin to sit quietly with each aspect and feel whether or not that is truly you or an overlay that you put on to keep your Self safe or apart or controlled in society.

Let us take humour for an example. Are you funny? Do you laugh a lot? Does humour find its way into your daily living? Do you think that humour is necessary or frivolous? Is humour "appropriate?" Are you funnier at home or at work? Are you never funny? Is life too hard? Look at this joy factor. Did you grow up in a house where laughter and joy were normally a part of everyday living or was it considered frivolous? Are you truly funny or not? Do you enjoy laughter? If you do not, it may be that it is not truly you, but rather the situations of your life that have caused you to not experience the joy of a good laugh or the appreciation of humour. It may not be who YOU are.

Take this with every thing on the list. Compassion or intimacy. Do those feel safe and secure to you? Are you wiling to allow people into your life to share it, explore it and experience it with you?

If you can begin to remove the masks of daily living you will become more alive. As you discover who is hiding under the camouflage of your current existence you will begin to feel more open, more free and more alive.

We leave you exposed and visible and alive.
Namaste

PAIN

Do you live with pain? It can be either physical or mental or psychic in nature. What do you drag through each day? What causes the pain? Many chalk it up to old age or lack of exercise, some are truly ill and have body pain associated with dis-ease and yet others carry the mental burden of pain. Pain could be a constant for you and you might not even be aware of it.

Make a list of painful thoughts you carry through your day. If you do not believe you have any, take a moment to analyze your thoughts. Do you think only loving and uplifting thoughts of your Self, your family, your friends or your co-workers? Do you praise your Self throughout the day for being the best you can be in any moment or do you analyze each move and find it lacking? How many of you have thoughts from events that happened long ago that you are still harbouring and rehashing and reworking? Do those thoughts stay with you to help you feel right or justified in your behaviours? Think of something you truly wanted or desired or felt entitled to have and remember what it is like not to have it. Does that make for a painful thought?

Most of you carry pain inducing thoughts with you every moment of every day. You are not beautiful enough, smart enough, thin enough, fit enough, rich enough, appreciated enough or whatever other blows of Self-defeating imagery you can manifest. Why? Do you enjoy the pain?

What would it be like to live without the burdens of these judgments and replaying of events out of your control? Peaceful and pain free would be our answer. Look at what you do that keeps you in pain. Besides the thoughts, perhaps it is your diet. You may be eating foods that cause you to have inflammation, upset or distress. You might even know what these foods are, but you continue to eat them in the "hopes" that one day it will not matter. This is not the case. Learn to listen to your body. Is that food, pill, drug or drink serving your body which houses your Soul which facilitates your living? Is your body being treated as it needs to be? Pain is not caused by the outside world most of the time, it is caused by your reaction to the outside world. The only thing you can control is your reaction to external forces. You choose to keep your Self in prison, in pain and in fear.

Take some time to sit in meditation and just clear your mind. Allow your Self to travel to the center of your being and into the void where nothing is everything and you can experience a few moments of bliss and pain free living. This is what was meant to be for you all. Sometimes the Soul craves the pain as it believes that it is healing. Perhaps it is, but for most of you it is just an addiction to something that keeps you from living the life you came to live. It keeps you from connecting to life joyously so that you can live fully and alive.

We leave you in peace.
Namaste

PERFECTION

What if you were told that right here, right now you could have perfection?

Would you believe it?

Would you want it?

The common answer is that you most certainly would want perfection. It is what you strive for, work at, long for and hope one day to realize. Perfection is different for each of you. For some it is the total immersion of Spirit with body, for others it could mean the perfect weight or health or relationship. It might just mean that your life would finally match your pictures of what life should look like to you.

So let us say that you would like to have the perfect body. What is the perfect body? Is it tall, thin, curvaceous, rock hard, muscled, strong, shapely, sturdy or useful? What represents perfection to you? We choose the physical since it is a focus of many and it is the vehicle for your Soul. What kind of hair would be perfect? What weight? Would it be a body with no aches and pains? Would it be physically fit and available for action at all times? What is perfection? If you could have that right now, would you take it? Would you be willing to have your Soul in alignment with the outward reflection of perfection? Perfection comes from joy, from living, from experience. It is a state of being in which there are no wants, fears, troubles or upsets. It is living in the void or bliss as we see it. It is without tensions or events that require you push back against issues. You would be flowing effortlessly through life. Are you truly willing to give up all your stories for this state of bliss?

We want you to really think about this offer. It would mean that how you think and feel right now, the way in which you view your Self and others would magically disappear and in its place would be just a perfect, peaceful Soul. This lightening rod trip to perfection and realization would leave out all the pitfalls, bumps, detours and uphill climbs called life.

Please, we urge you to think about how invested you are in the life you have right now. How willing are you to change one thing about your way of being in the pursuit of a life of bliss? Are you willing to give up one friend or acquaintance that does not serve your road to perfection? Can you give up one habit that does not serve your physical needs or keeps you from having health? Are you willing to look at your Self honestly – with brutal honesty and see your foibles, failures, missteps as you so honestly and harshly judge others? If you will try just one thing that keeps you from perfection and remove it from your life, then you will have taken the first step. All great journeys begin with the first step.

We leave you in peace.
Namaste

INSIGHT

Do you listen to your own insight?

Do you follow your gut?

Do you follow your heart?

Do you heed what you hear or feel
in a given circumstance?

Do you give credence to your instincts?

Most of you have insights on a regular basis. You sense danger or uneasiness. You also sense connection and warmth when meeting new people or being in new circumstances. The bigger question is do you trust your Self with these signs or signals? Now some of you may have a heightened sense of fear or doom or pessimism which will cloud your own true feelings and so this may be difficult to read. Also, you may discount your premonitions, sensations and insights because you have never considered that you possess such a gift, but you all do on some level.

How do you go about cultivating this aspect of your being? We would always recommend meditation first because this is a state of being in which you are in suspended animation for a period of time. You are in quiet and nothingness. As you begin to learn to conquer your thoughts and their power, you begin to let go of much of your resistance to the journey inward to your Soul. In this journey you begin to trust your Self to find the right footing to take you safely along the journey. Trust is a big part of developing insight. You need to trust that you are able to do it and then trust that what you are hearing is not manufactured by you or your fears talking. It truly is easier than it sounds but you must begin by the practice and dedication to meditation on a regular and hopefully daily basis.

One of the things that insight gives to you is a much less fearless way of living. It helps you realize that you are not alone. The guidance and mentoring that you have so long sought outside of your Self becomes an integral part of you. You become a Self-contained vessel that can better navigate the shoals of your life. You begin to create a roadmap to living in peace, joy and calm. When you give up the struggle of trying to "get it" and you relax into the possibility of knowing that life will work for you, it removes a huge proportion of the stress and worry that have permeated your life up to now.

Please do not worry that you will turn into a noodle of disconnected calm and not be able to function. We promise that all of your intellect will be available to you still, but it will be more accessible through calm. Think of it again in terms of calm water and white water. Which would you rather be in most of the time? Yes, white water is exhilarating and fun and challenging and dangerous and humans enjoy risk to a certain extent, but the calm waters offer respite from the noise and the tumult.

Begin the road to insight five minutes at a time at least three days a week. View it as an exercise program for your Soul. Commit to the practice of making your mind and true being more fit, more firm and more aware so that you can enjoy the beauty of true insight. Insight that you provide for you, about you and within you.

We leave you in peace.
Namaste

MOTIVATION

What motivates you?

What makes you spring into action, to fully embrace life or projects or people?

Do you have a longing in your heart or are you a being that wishes things were different?

What would motivate you to begin the change?

Observation is a good way to work on motivation. Notice your Self as you observe life around you. Think about the thing or things that you would like to be different in your life. Pick one or two and work with them for a few days. Would you like to be more fit? Would you like to be more at peace? Would you like to be in love? What is it that you believe you lack right now? Pick the two things and just bring them into your conscious awareness. By this we mean that you need to say,

"I would like _______ to be different"

or

"I would like to act differently with ______."

Now over the course of the next few days begin to notice how often circumstances or people or life puts examples of those things in front of you. Notice your reaction to them. Are you jealous of others that have these things? Are you envious? Do you find you are resentful that others can have this and you cannot? How about noticing that people to whom you previously might have felt superior are now doing this thing you have not achieved? How does that make you feel?

Motivation comes from the Soul's realization that it wants to change. It usually has to reach the peak of frustration or upset or sadness or anger before you will put into place the things you need to do in order to facilitate a change in your life. Most of you want things to change as you lie in front of the TV or you read a book or drink a beer. Change is an action word and if you are not in action you are not in change. Yes, it can be a mental shift in perception but you have to be motivated to give up your previous belief system, thought patterns and victimhood in order to make the shift mentally. You have to realize that the thoughts and ways of being that you have are not serving you. Do not despair, for they may have served you at one time but circumstances and life have put you more in a place of inertia than a place of action.

We are not asking for you to change anything TODAY or RIGHT NOW, we are only suggesting that you look at what you long for and begin to have rather than not have.

We leave you highly motivated and in love with life.
Namaste

FEAR

We come back to fear. It is such a pervasive emotion for the human condition. It permeates the existence of most of you and controls the outcome of your lives. It stops free will and joy from manifesting as it should. There are certain basic aspects of fear that are good for you as they protect you from hazards or pitfalls. That is the primal form of fear. It is a basic instinct.

Fear only becomes a problem when you allow it to color your decisions, your actions and your lives. You begin to fear new things coming into your life. You begin to fear that you have "gotten it wrong" or "made a mistake" and now something unseen and horrible will befall you. The only thing that is horrible is that your mind is taking you on a journey of fear. This journey will affect your body, your being and your relationship with life. It will stop you from living fully and fearlessly. It will stop you from connecting with life on many levels.

Think of something that recently caused you fear or that constantly causes you fear. It could be a health issue or job issue or relationship issue or simply a personal safety issue. Sit with this "fearful" thing for a few moments. Try to follow the fear backwards to its source. What is causing the fear or what is it that you are fearful about? Is it being lonely, being harmed, being made fun of or being singled out? What is the fear? Then spend a few moments on how this fear makes you feel in your body. Does it enliven you or make you tense? Does it open you up or does it shut you down. If the event is something that is already in the past, was the outcome as you expected? To put it another way, was it worth the fear? As we have said many times, there is very little that you control, but it is important to remember that you control your reaction to life.

That is the one thing that is always in your control. If you are reacting from joy, you are expansive and in possibility. If you are reacting from fear you are shut down and isolated. We are not advocating giving up being cautious about life, but there is a difference between caution and fear. If you take a few moments you can run a quick list of things that frighten you. Now for some it might be better for us to list this as things that you find upsetting or disappointing or life events that you do not like such as a health issue. You may not describe your reaction to it as fear, but rather you feel discomfort or unease about it.

The fear we are describing does not have to be gripping or gut-wrenching, but it can be as simple as a low level disturbance that keeps you from having what you want or acting on information that is given to you. Let us liken this to knowing you have to make a phone call and you do not particularly want to make the call and so you postpone it and then you postpone it again and you continue to do so until this simple phone call becomes huge or long overdue and now it is HUGE that you have not called and you still have to do it.

The beginning of eradicating fear is simply being ready to face the future and do the work and get it done. If you do it while it is fresh and new it is manageable, but as you let it build it becomes almost insurmountable and bigger than you can handle. This has usually been created in your mind. So again, travel back to the source, remember it as it was at the beginning and jump into the stream of life and swim.

We leave you fearlessly swimming in the river of life.
Namaste

DEDICATION

How committed are you to living life fully?

How willing are you to do what it takes to live the life you were meant to live?

Being committed or dedicated to a process is necessary for you to begin the journey toward reclaiming your Self. Like in all things that require focus and attention, it is necessary to refocus your actions and attention on the things that will move you along the path to your destination. This means that behaviours, people, circumstances that may have been occurring in your life will have to shift or alter or change. It means a "rededication" to the ways of living that will help you to realize Self. The journey requires that you look in the mirror of your Soul and see the reflections, begin to identify the distortion and cut some of the refraction. It is the marshalling of your energy, psyche and Soul into a team that is dedicated to the realization of Self.

Who are you?
What do you want?
Where are you going?

Those are the questions that so many of you seek whether fervently or quietly or subconsciously. Some people wonder this in different ways throughout their life. In the early years you wonder who you are supposed to be, what are you supposed to do? The middle years are spent wondering, "Is this what I am supposed to be doing and is this what I want?" The later years are spent pondering where have you been and is it too late to change. Will you ever know what to do and where to go? The answers are always yes and yet not knowing makes the journey more interesting on many levels.

The key during all stages of life is to live each day fully and as fearlessly as possible. If you do that and you remain present in the moments of life you will find the journey to be interesting, intriguing and life affirming. If you live your life half asleep, you may find the journey boring, tiresome, difficult or hard. It is only a journey and you get out of it only what you put into it.

So we ask again, how dedicated are you to making the journey lively, alive and full of joy? Will you willingly allow that being alive is the first step? Being alive and joyful does not negate being a hard working person and having goals and focus that are very much a part of living. It does however require that you find a balance that includes work, play, Spiritual experiences and intimacy with other human beings. Intimacy requires vulnerability and that requires trust.

Think about trust and we leave you in joy.
Namaste

DESPAIR

Of what do you despair?

What seems so hopeless in your life that you cannot bring your Self back to a place of limitless possibility?

Who told you that it was not possible?

Our guess is that most of you have been told it is not possible by your own minds. Now your minds may have been abetted by programming, thoughts or comments from others, but it is your choice to believe them. Most of you work on a system of external beliefs that you then internalize. What does that mean? You come into this world with certain aspects in place and then it is your environment coupled with the strength of your Soul that begins to direct your life. How much do you care about YOU? How important are YOU to the process?

Let us take programming. Did someone tell you that you were ugly or fat or stupid or worthless? If so, who? Why did you let that person's opinion matter more than your own? Did you have no opinion of your own? What is beauty, what is intellect, what is the perfect body for YOU? Those are the questions that you must ask. Then you need to ask the most important question – Who are you really? What does your Soul look like? Can your Soul be too fat or too thin or ugly or stupid? No, because your Soul does not really have human traits. Your Soul is a wonderful bright light that illuminates your being. It gives you grace, elegance, purpose and meaning, but most of you have no idea how beautiful and magnificent a Soul you possess.

Who are you?

Answer that question in writing. You can write full sentences or you can write just words, but describe your Self. Do it quickly and then review what you believe to be true about your Self. Notice the words and descriptions that you use. What do you feel like as you read those words? Next determine if those are truly your words or are they again what you have been told and have come to believe? When you hear the negative things in your head about your Self, whose voice or voices are they? Are they parents or other family, teachers, spouses, co-workers, friends, children from your school days – Who is telling you all of these things? More importantly why do you believe them?

If you are measuring up to your dreams and ideals, then you have perhaps conquered most of the voices, if you are living in despair that you will never have what you want, we would tell you that it is time to lose the negative Self-talk. Give it back to the people from whence it originally came and get on with a life that listens to your Soul and not your head. Spend time each day in meditation and quiet so that you can begin to get the rhythms of living life as you were truly meant to be.

We leave in joy.
Namaste

COMMITMENT

To what are you willing to commit? By this we mean truly commit – fully, thoroughly, completely and Spiritually. Most of you say you are committed to something and then somewhere along the line you give up or stop or feel that is enough or move your attention to another project or idea. In essence you stop before you reach the goal or the end or the point of whatever it was that initially took your attention.

Why do you stop?
Is it too hard?
Does it not match your pictures?
Do you really not want the thing or goal to which you committed?

Let us take weight. Many of you bemoan that you are not the right weight yet you continue to eat and sit in chairs and eat improper nutrition. You bemoan your fate, yet you do not want to give up or change anything about your condition. You might go on a diet but diets are short term unless you completely change your way of being with food. Anyone can starve themselves for a while. Anyone can give up non-nutritional foods for a short period but if you continue to crave them, long for them, wish for them, you will ultimately return to them. So perhaps your goals are not clearly defined. If you "wish" you were thinner than you will not be because as we have said many times, wishing does not have much energy.

Let us take other examples as well before we discuss the process. Let us say you drink too much, work too much or don't work hard enough. Maybe you want to buy a house or have a partner or bear children. You say these are goals, but are you committed to the process of having what you want?

Having what you want is about claiming it for your Self. You need to truly be aligned with your goals and dreams. They must have determination behind them otherwise they are just thoughts or wishes. Commitment means sticking with your decisions even when it is not easy or convenient or simple or mainstream. Commitment is continuing even in the face of adversity, ridicule, coercion or distain. Commitment is knowing that what you are doing is for your best purpose in living. A commitment is your word that you will run the race and reach the goal line. You may fall down on the way there. You may trip and stumble, you may sit down and take some time out and you will most certainly question your decision to go down this path, but commitment keeps you honest and directed and intentional in your living.

Many people are getting married or forming relationships. When they do not match your pictures or they are not as pretty as you wanted or they are hard or annoying or difficult, many of you want to leave. You think that they are like clothing you can try on and cast aside when they have a stain or a tear or are faded. This is not true. Now we realize that it takes two people or more in relationship to make things work, but our question to you is how committed are YOU to making this work. This does not mean subjugating your Self or living with abuse, but rather demanding what you believe is possible for both people concerned. It is calling forth another to be in commitment with the promises and vows taken. It is not always your way that is best and even it if is, it is not always your way that will triumph.

So again, look at what you claim or are committed to and analyze that level of commitment. If the goal is more important than all the “things” in the way, then you can truly commit and begin your journey to joy, love and enlightenment

We leave in love.
Namaste

VISIT

Have you ever just sat in the core of your being? It is the void that we have called Bliss before. It is nothing and everything all in one. It is complete silence and the roar of a thousand voices.

It is calm.
It is nothing.
It is you.

Do you believe that you are a void of calm nothingness? As you travel through your days of upset, upheaval, thoughts, emotions and travails do you realize that they are all trappings or coverings for this true Self – this Void?

Most of you want to avoid the Void. You have concerns or fears that are related to being just alone with your Self, without your stories, trappings and distortions. There is a fear of being just completely silent and alone and floating peacefully on a cloud of perfection. You are all perfect. It is the distortions that you carry and allow other people to mirror at you that causes your unrest. In the silence of Self there is nothing wrong, there is nothing to fix, there is nothing but there is everything. It is a place of contentment, joy, possibility, love and peace. It resides inside of you – not outside. It is like a wonderful space capsule that will take you to galaxies far, far away, but you never have to leave home. It is a pure drop of elixir that answers all questions and begs none. It is knowing and it is simply – Being. It is not "human" being it is just Being.

Each of you has within you the ability to travel to this space daily. It brings you respite from the winds of living and yet most of you do not want to take the time or practice to be at peace within. You want peace without. You want world peace, but not Self peace. You rail against circumstances that cause heartache and loss and you harbour anger or grief about it.

Where do you go for peace? Is it illusive to you? It is not but a short journey into your Self and the permission to sit there and rest with no thoughts, desires or needs other than complete silence and peace. Take the time to begin learning the path to this place. The day of discovery will be one of great joy and amusement. It will be home.

We leave you in peace and love
Namaste

CONTENTMENT

Loving What Is!
It Is What It Is!
Let It Be!

These are all phrases used in your vernacular to describe how it is easier to be content with where you are in the moment rather than constantly railing against what you do not have or desire. How annoying are those phrases to you? Do they offer you peace or irritation? Many of you think that if you are not content with something you need to be in anger or upheaval about it. Many of you believe that upheaval foments changes and to a certain extent it does, but it leaves the fomenters in a state of anger and agitation. You can change the world through anger or you can change it through acceptance.

When you accept that life is how it is right now in this moment; you release tension, upset, unhappiness and anger. You can then allow that something else can fill up that space. If you protest from a place of peace and calm it is far more powerful than if you protest from a place of agitation. It is hard for forces to react against you if you refuse to react back. Now we could discuss this on a world peace level or give examples of peaceful protest such as Gandhi, but we are here actually to assist you in the peaceful protest within your own life.

At what are you angry? What about your life frustrates you or upsets you or annoys? What can you not love right now just as it is? If you love something it can transform. This happens because you give it fertile ground in which to blossom and flower and thrive. If the soil of your heart is full of anger, upset, resentment and judgment; it is not a healthy soil in which to grow contentment, love and prosperity. You are choking off the nutrients that are required to allow life to thrive within you.

Tension causes "dis"ease, it causes pain, it causes sleeplessness, it causes disharmony. Take a moment and think about how you feel when you are angry with another person. It does not have to be "big" anger, but just mild annoyance. How do you feel? We do not care if that person deserves it or earned it or created it, we are concerned with how you feel. Are you at ease, is your breathing normal? Can you relax and laugh at something that is funny or inane in that moment or do you keep laughter from you because someone else does not deserve your happiness? Think about what you are doing. You are robbing your Self of joy every time you become annoyed or angry with another. More importantly you are robbing your Self of joy every time you are not in harmony with loving your Self just as you are in this moment.

Life is a series of events – some are good and some are bad and some are easy and some are hard and some are fun and some are boring. Being human is a life of contrasts; it is your reaction to the contrast that makes the difference. Many of you have lost loved ones, perhaps in unfair circumstances. Does your anger bring them back or does it rob you of living and enjoying this life with all the other people that surround you? If you allow your Self to be forlorn then you are robbing those around you of your full presence. You have given up a part of you to life. Reclaim YOU. Find the ecstasy that is available through breath and breathing. Find the true source of contentment and then live in a place of bliss. It is very near at hand, even if you think it is far away.

We leave in joy and possibility.
Namaste

EASE

What do you think of when you hear the word Graceful?

Does it evoke a sense of ease, or floating effortlessly through a room or through life?

Do you move easily through life?

If you were to liken your approach to moving through life to a type of walking, what would it be? Would it be slow and ponderous steps? Would it be lively and flitting types of movements? Would you sprint? Perhaps you would slowly stroll through, stopping along the way to rest or enjoy nature. Are you exhausted by life? At the end of the day do you fall into bed with no energy having spent the day dragging your thoughts, worries, concerns and Self judgment with you? Do you want to escape life or embrace it? Please sit and analyze your physical approach to living. Again, are there weights attached to you or do you fly through the day with joy? What are you choosing?

The burdens of your life are imaginary. Now this is a statement that will upset many of you for you will rush to give us the evidence that your life is hard or filled with challenges or burdens that we can know nothing about. We are not arguing that your lives are full of challenges and events that may be time consuming or more time consuming than other people. You may live with people who are ill or you may have children that are causing ripples in the surface of your life, but again we return to the point that it is your reaction to those situations that cause your upsets, not the situations. We are also not telling you to be devoid of emotion or caring, but rather to assess the importance you attach to certain things. Just observe life around you. There are people in similar circumstances to yours and each of them reacts differently. Some move joyously through it, some are silent martyrs, some rant and rave and carry on about their burdens and others you might never know what burdens they carry. Is any one approach the best or the "right" one? No, but it does give you perspective when you observe the commonality of your unique situation.

Try for one day to choose ease. This means that for that day you put down the burden of the world that you believe you must carry on your shoulders. You trust those around you to behave or function without your constant worry and supervision. You allow each human being to be human and that would include your Self. Make a list of the things that you honestly, truly have to do. Do not include supervision of others or more aptly put, control. Do just what is necessary to get through your day. If this means driving children to school, then drive them, but do so joyfully or at least with no resistance. If you work, do the tasks that are associated with your job, do not worry about anyone else's performance; just a day doing your job and your job only. Feel what it is like to not be the commander of the universe for one day. Notice the places that are more restful and notice the ones that are causing you stress because your habit is to control or interfere. Notice any changes in your mood or energy level. Try to constantly remove your mind from "other people" and what they should or should not be doing. Just live happily in the bubble called your life.

Try it for one day and see what happens and then begin to slowly put it into play in your everyday life. Be in control of you, be in happiness with you and be at ease with life.

We leave you easily.
Namaste

WORK

Are you willing to do the work?

Many of you are dedicated or hard workers. You toil endlessly with the daily tasks of life. You are dedicated to your jobs, your families and the mundane tasks of living such as cleaning, chores and activities of living. What work do you do for your Soul?

How much time do you give each day or even each week to the betterment or care of your Soul? Do you meditate daily? Can you find the five minutes per day that we recommend as your starting point? Can you find fifteen minutes each day to move your life's journey further down the path to enlightenment or are you too busy doing all the other work? Is a clean house worth more than your Soul? Is the television program you are watching better for you than a journey to the center of your being? Many of you want to just "relax" when you get home because your day has been so stressful. How do you relax? Do you drink or try to numb out in some way? Do you eat? Do you sit in front of the television or the computer and just travel outside of your Self?

Here is a secret – Listen closely – the journey into your Self is far more rewarding and relaxing than anything that you can find outside of your Self. The journey to the center of you is exquisite and magical and enlightening and fun-filled and explosive. A few minutes sitting in the void is worth all the other things that you might consider doing to "relax." It is a journey to the reclamation of your being. It is the connection of body and Soul. It is Self realization, but are you willing to do the work? It is not always easy to begin the journey to meditation and silence. You are programmed to be noisy. Your society is noisy. The messages are all about going outside of your Self to find joy. If you are thinner, have no wrinkles, have a fabulous job, lots of money, lots of things then you will have "Nirvana." Surprise, Nirvana is within, not "with out." Take an assessment of all the mindless things that you spend your time on. The worries about how you look, your bills, how you are perceived in the world. How do you perceive your Self? Are you only reflected in other people's vision of you? Do you need external validation to make you worthwhile?

Travel in and find the validation you desire. Travel in and find the peace you crave. Travel in and find your Self.

We leave quietly and in love.
Namaste

JOY

Can you find joy in small things?

Can you find the joy that exists in everyday life?

Can you overcome your beliefs that life is hard
and focus on the joy of living?

Joy is an elusive thing for most of you. You can probably count on your hands, without needing your toes, the number of truly joyful times you have experienced lately. Joy is a natural state. Let that statement settle in for you.

Joy is a natural state of being.

God fills your hearts and you can be in joy. You can have joy even in great sadness if you so choose. Let us say that you lost a loved one recently. Society tells you that you are grieving and you therefore must be sad all of the time and depressed by this loss. Why? Yes, they are no longer with you in the physical sense and that is a difficult concept to move your minds around, but their Spirit is always with you. That is a joyful thing. The fact that you cannot manifest them in a physical sense is not the worst thing that could happened. Let us say that it was a relative that lived far away from you. Perhaps you talked to them on the phone or communicated with them in writing. Now suddenly they are gone and you are saddened. You wish that they could return so that you might have the hope of seeing them again, but is this logical? They were not a part of your everyday world and now you are allowing your everyday existence to be colored by their passing. They are still with you. You can know that they never leave you and therefore, while not physical, they are not far.

So as you think of them, find joy in your heart rather than sadness or pain. Choose joy over upset.

Let us now say that you are working some place that is not "fun" all of the time. You do not enjoy the environment, yet you continue to stay there for whatever your reason may be. If you must stay there, why do you not choose joy rather than upset? Why do you allow that you must choose unhappiness rather than joy? If you can be more joyful in the situation, it will begin to transform because the energy that you are putting into the situation is one of uplifting and lighter movement. If you remain heavy and sad and angry around the project or job or situation, it has more difficulty transforming for in a way you are solidifying it rather than setting it free.

Joy sets you free. It allows your Spirit to soar and therefore it allows you to create, imagine, laugh and be free.

Choose Freedom.
Choose Laughter.
Choose Joy.

We leave you joyfully.
Namaste

LOVE

In the end there is only love, but it is true of the beginning as well. Love is the energy that permeates existence. Love is the energy that drives human existence and yet you so often let go of it, or alter it or place conditions upon it so that you can limit the amount of love you are willing to receive and give. For some reason you believe that love is not safe. What is love to you? Is it a limited quantity of affection you choose to rain upon others? Is it a limitless emotion that when given freely and constantly can alter lives and move mountains?

You clamor for peace, for fairness, for justice and yet you control love. You withhold love because someone has been rude or bad or ugly or has not in some way matched your pictures. You confuse love with forgiveness, with understanding, with almost every other emotion. So do many people. You believe if you show too much love to someone they will take advantage of you. Sit for a moment and think about how many kinds of love you believe there are in the world. Love thy neighbor as you love thy Self seems to be one. There is parental or child/parent love. There is the love of friends and relatives. There is passionate, sexual love. There is a love of animals. There is the love of God or whatever Spirit manifestation you choose. How about love of your fellow man? How good are you at that one?

Every time you find fault in another you are finding fault in your Self. Yes, that is an absolutely true statement. Do not try to justify or mitigate or deny the truth of that statement.

Every time you find fault in another, you are finding fault in your Self.

Please sit with that for a moment. When you cannot express love and compassion for another being, you are not expressing love or compassion for your Self. Every judgment you rain upon another is a judgment about you. As you begin to understand this you will begin to see how most of you live your life in Self abuse and Self punishment. Someone didn't do today something you wanted them to do. What did you not do today that you wanted to do, thought you should do or wished you had done? Someone is unkind to you or does not match your pictures. What did you do today that was thoughtless, unkind or unconscious? As Jesus said, "Let he who is without sin be the first to cast a stone." How many stones do you cast at others when you are just as deserving?

If you can learn to love your Self and we mean deep down, dirty, full-on loving your Self without condition, without judgment and without fear, then you can begin to love those outside of you and then this world will begin to transform and become the Eden it was meant to be.

All you need is love - dum, de, dum, dum, dum.

We leave in love.
Namaste

TRANSFORMATON

What does it mean to be transformed?
What do you want to transform?

If you have identified that which does not make you happy and you wish it to be different, how will you go about this task? What is the difference between transformation and dissatisfaction? In order to transform, you must be fully committed to the process. It is a commitment that is not to be taken lightly. It is a journey in which you need to find that which you truly want and need to transform. For most of you it is a surface thing that first catches your attention. You might want to be happier, or more fit or have better relationships. It could be driven by loneliness or disgust or frustration. You can begin to change many things on a very shallow level. How many of you dieted and lost weight and loved your look, only to gain the weight back? How many of you have "allowed" a relationship to enter your life, perhaps after a long hiatus and been enamoured of the situation and then at some point found your Self back at the same problems you had before.? How many of you can start a project and give it a lot of energy but quit right before it is done? These are all examples of how you change behaviours or situations for a temporary time but you do not transform the factors that keep you from going back.

Transformation means that you must get to the root or roots of the problem or problems. You must dig deeply into your Soul or your psyche and find the triggers, obstacles and hurdles to having the life you desire and deserve. If you have an eating problem, what triggers the issue? It is easy to say that you crave foods or don't know how to eat well or do not exercise, but why? You must follow the thread backwards to find the source. It is perhaps easy to blame others. Take relationship issues, perhaps you did not come from a home that modeled warm and loving relationships, or you have had a bad relationship and now you don't trust. Okay, but what is the source of the distrust? Is it that you distrust others or do you distrust your Self? The answer is your Self. Something about your Self is out of alignment and that is what needs to be transformed. You all want something outside of your Self to change or modify and then you will be transformed, but the journey begins with you. Everything begins with you and once you realize that Self is what matters and Self is what needs transformation and Self is where the healing occurs, then you can begin the journey to the transformation of the overlying beliefs that you hold on to that are keeping your Self from joy from life and from love.

Become your own transformer and you will have unbounded energy.

We leave energetically.
Namaste

FOCUS

How focused are you?

Do you have singleness of purpose?

Are you able to concentrate on the things that matter the most?

Can you define the things that matter most?

Many of you flit from thing to thing. You have lives that are filled with a lot of commitments, "must dos" and "must haves." This causes you to be running from place to place and not being able to stay focused on the things that truly matter. As always we return to meditation. How willing are you to take five minutes, just five minutes, per day to sit quietly and focus your attentions within rather than without? Can you sit peacefully for five minutes and not think of all the other things that you should or could be doing? What would it be like for you to sit with nothing but quiet? The power of silence is enormous. It removes the day-to-day chatter of living and all the things that you believe to be so important are reduced to silence.

Just as we have discussed about the void, in nothingness is everything. Silence allows you to be at peace. Once you are at peace you can begin to listen to the guidance, love, education and insights that are waiting for you in the void. You all claim to want guidance. Many of you seek it outside of your Self with psychics, readers, astrology or whatever mode, but you have within you - available for free - many of the answers you seek. If you can focus inward your attentions, you will begin to discern the answers to many of your questions. You will begin to realize that most of your questions do not really need an answer, but rather the silence of the void will relieve your need for many of these questions.

"Less is more," is a phrase that many of you have heard. This is very true. The less you do, the more you have available to you. What if you did not over plan your days with things, meetings, people, or commitments? What would that be like? The more you choose peace over chaos, the more clear your life will become. As you begin to take the time for your Self rather than exhausting your Self in activities, you will see that you have more of your Self to share. This right now does not make sense to you because you are exhausting your Self by racing from pillar to post doing, doing, doing. Most of you are running away from your Self rather than to it. There is nothing to fear in going within. There is nothing to harm you within. There is nothing but bliss within you and it can be accessed at any time. So go within and find the solitude, the answers and the joy awaiting you.

We leave you peacefully.
Namaste

SELF SABOTAGE

Most of life is Self sabotage. You all make up stories about how life is not working for you and how you are victimized in some way by life, but if you truly look at the situation you will see that it is YOU or Self that keeps you from having what you want. We do not say this to be punitive or difficult, but rather to point out that most of life is caused by Self denial or abuse or sabotage.

Let us say that you are in a relationship and that relationship is not as you like. As the other person does not transform, you become more agitated and upset. They are not being the best they can be and they are not changing for you. If they really loved you, if they really cared for you, if they were not so Selfish they wou.......... And if and if and if. Most people are living their lives and they are not changing or being more generous or whatever the problem is because they do not want to change their inner being, they do not want to find their true Self. It fascinates us how much this annoys all of you, for are ***you*** willing to find your "true" inner Self? Are you willing to do the work that will set you free and allow you to live a life unfettered with worries, upsets, concerns and controls? Are you willing to give up that which causes you to worry about things? Are you willing to give up that which causes you to try to control the chaos of life? Are you willing to change your eating habits to have better health? Are you willing to change your exercise program to better suit fitness? Are you willing to give up drinking alcohol for better health?

Every time you begin to judge another for their seeming reluctance to change "for the better" because you can see how much better it would be for them, stop and really think about what you need to change in you.

Always begin to till your own garden first. Spending time worrying about how someone else "needs" to change is time spent away from healing your Self and becoming the best possible human being you know how to be.

This is a joyful journey, this thing called Life. It is full of lessons, and laughter and love and adventure, but as long as you label it all as hard, or ugly or stupid or boring or a struggle, it will be for you. It is a journey to Self that can take you to realms undreamed. You have to be willing to let go of changing the world and begin at home. Think about great people who have begun the steps to Spirituality and that has allowed them to open their Souls into larger and larger spaces so that they can create more joy, abundance and understanding in this world. Begin the journey your Self desires and you will be amazed whom you find walking along the path with you.

We leave in hope.
Namaste

POSSIBILITY

What would you like to be possible today?

What thing or feeling or event would you like to have occur?

What is possible?

Is possibility limited?

Yes, it often is to your imagination. Most of you dream and think and wish for things and it is within in a very limited scope. You dream of things that would make your Spirits soar, or so you think and then you limit the possibility of their occurring.

Step away from the dreams and hopes and wishes. Make them, send them out into the ethers of time and then step away. Possibility occurs in a vacuum or in the Void. If you are pressed up tight against it you cannot allow for it to happen. Think about standing at a window. If your face is pressed up against the glass, can you see the entire scene? Step back from the window and look again at the view, how much more is there? It is in the asking and releasing of the outcome that possibility occurs. The gifts available are far greater than those you imagine.

This brings us to trust. Do you trust that good things will occur? We label them as “good” today for your benefit for many of you spend your time in good and bad, happy and sad, fair and unfair. So do you trust that “good” things can occur without your daily, minute-to-minute management? Trust and possibility go hand-in-hand.

The next part of having life work as you want is to ask, let go, trust and then be ready to say YES when opportunity arises. Saying Yes is an art. It does not come easily to most of you. You might protest, but think about it. How often do you spontaneously say Yes - without hesitation, thought or worries? Do you openly offer your Self to the world and to opportunity or do you think – "No, I don't have time." or "No, I don't think I can do that." or "No I am not ready." You are always ready. Remember this phrase:

You are always ready

Even when you think you are not, you are because in that moment miracles can happen. In the Yes. In the stepping into a space that you do not yet think you are ready for, miracles and possibility occur. Now, maybe you are not loved for the thing you do in that moment, but just the act of stepping into the energy of Yes makes things begin to transform. Failure, as you all label it, is just a way of finding out what not to do. It is a tool, not an end in it-Self.

Become Yes
Become Transformation
Become Possibility

We leave you in a world of limitless possibility.
Namaste

CURIOSITY

How curious are you? Do you spend a lot of time wondering about other people's business, motivations, actions or lives? Do you read magazines or papers that delve into others' lives so that you can live vicariously through their exploits? Do you revel in famous or rich people's failings or missteps? Do you feel entitled to see their children or their homes? What makes you so curious about others? Is it a lack of your own life or perceived inferiority? Do you enjoy the gossip because it makes you feel that maybe their lives are not perfect either!!?

Curiosity is a wonderful state. It makes you explore the intricacies of life, if that is how you choose to use it. It is where you spend your curiosity that is of concern to us. Are you curious what it would feel like to sit quietly in a blissful state of nothingness and feel your Spirit/Soul soar to heights unknown? Are you curious how you could develop your Soul's journey so that you could maximize the adventure of life? Are you curious about your gifts and ability to have insights? Do you want to know how to eat better, live better, love more? Those are things that should make you all curious. Many of you claim that you are wanting or desiring these things and yet you continue down this path of ignorance. Please do not be insulted by the use of that word, we mean it as an example of non-curiosity, not intellect. Within you lies a world that is so beautiful and magnificent that you cannot imagine the vistas that you would see and yet you choose to stay a tourist that only visits the borders of living.

Life is holistic. It occurs inside and outside of you. The external is easily accessible to you all. You open your eyes or your ears or any of your senses and you can fully experience what you want. That is if you choose to fully experience it. We find that you limit your Selves in the external as well as the internal world. Now we are not preaching for excesses in food, drink or physical exertion, but we are saying that many of you limit the experiences of life to keep your Selves "safe." Perhaps this is why you become voyeuristically interested in the lives of celebrities and the famous. Perhaps this is why you revel in the reality programs because the "unreality" of those programs allows you to not journey very far out of your comfort zone. You can sit in your living rooms and watch other people risk their reputation, overcome their fears, put themselves on the line for their dreams and that is enough.

Is it? Is it enough to watch life happening from the sidelines? We think that as you watch "real" people on television you begin to feel that you wish you could have all those things as well. Maybe a record contract or a movie contract or win a million dollars if you can survive on an island. If you could do any of those things then – THEN - your life would be worth living. This is nonsense and you are all being lulled into a false sense of security and dreams. Get curious about your own life. Take the risk of finding out who you are and what makes you tick. Journey into the deepest, darkest places within your Self and find the magnificent brilliance of your being. Be curious about YOUR life, not just life.

We leave you seeking
Namaste

DIS-EASE

How many of you have experienced an illness or dis-ease that has caused you to reevaluate your life and how it is lived? Perhaps the illness has not even been your own, but rather that of a family member or close friend. How do you treat your body? How do you honor the vehicle that carries your Soul about in this life? Do you feed it the best foods you can and in the right quantities? Do you keep any drink to a minimum? Do you exercise your body in some way on a daily basis?

For many of you this is not the case. You go through the day putting in bad fuel in the form of food, drink, drugs, cigarettes and sugar and then wonder why you do not have the energy or the body you desire. Others of you starve the body in the hopes of being seen as slim or perfectly fit, yet how can a body be fit if you are not nourishing it with nutrients that build? There is no one way that anyone should live, but it needs to be noted that proper nutrition and diet is the key to feeling the best you can feel in the body you have. There are all types of bodies and each has its own requirements, but the basics remain.

Live a life of low stress. How? Your lives are full of things to do and places to be and work that "must" be done. You place enormous stresses upon your Self and then wonder why you are tired and out of sorts. Fatigue is a leading cause of dis-ease. Fatigue is not handled only by sleep, but also by the calming of the mental aspects of life. If you are not allowing for quiet to enter your mind, you will have constant thoughts that exhaust and debilitate you. We ask you to notice how quickly your mind races on a given day or maybe just for an hour long period. How many thoughts and how many of them are positive and uplifting? Listen to how you speak to your Self.

Find time for love. Now we do not mean that this is a partnered relationship type of love, but rather that you allow for love to be a part of your daily living. The most important person that you can love is YOU. How many of you can say that you lovingly treat your Self? What does lovingly treat your Self mean? It means that you find the time to listen to what you truly want and need. You do not push off your needs with beliefs that everyone else's needs come before yours. You listen to your body and your mind to find that which would love and support you. Just you. For if you are lovingly supported, you will begin to find that you have more energy and strength to deal with the daily storms of living. Martyrdom has never worked and it causes great resentment from those that surround you.

So, to return to the original message of the day, if you have some sort of dis-ease in your body or person take some time to analyze what may have contributed to the arrival of such a problem. Look again at nutrition, environment and mental status and analyze where you might be able to make some changes that would facilitate and happier and healthier body.

We leave in health and love.
Namaste

BELIEVING

Do you believe in your Self?

Do you believe that you are enough,
just as you are right now?

Do you believe that you have within you the
capability to know, be and achieve that
which you came here to do?

Believe

We hear many of you wrestle with the concept of God or religion or belief. How can you believe in something you cannot see or touch or feel? So, if believing in something that is unseen, unheard and untouched is difficult, can you believe in you? You are here right now. You are solid and concrete. You can have a daily dialogue with your Self and become intimate, but do you? Will you?

Believing in your Self is not so simple. First you need to realize that you have within you right now, the ability to know who you are and to fully realize your potential. The sounds of protest are overwhelming as we state this fact. The answer is within you. The magic potion or secret or tenet you seek or desire is within. That is where the journey must lead - to the core of your being!

Again, you seek the external when the internal is the location of your dreams, hopes, wishes and desires. Quiet moments of meditation will begin to help you move along the path to enlightenment and with enlightenment comes freedom. Freedom from worry, control and pain. If you realize your true

Self and nurture it, amazing things can occur for you that you never before thought possible. You just have to listen, learn, and then begin the steps along the path that will lead to the places you have desired. The first step is believing it can be so.

We leave you in contemplation of belief.
Namaste

LOVE

This is a topic so many of you long for, worry about, analyze and desire. Why do you think there is a scarcity of love? It abounds about you at all times. It is available to each and every one of you right now in this moment, but you do not reach out for it because you have too many constraints. It must come from this person or that person. It must look like this. It must be a certain way and just that way. It must be romantic. It must be unconditional. It must be controllable. It must be what?

Love is a condition of peace, inclusion, freedom, support, care and connection. Love is not sex. Love is not control. Love is not having everything you want right now. You cannot make others behave in loving and warm ways to you if they choose not to express love. Love is a natural condition that is warped and twisted and manipulated by the human condition. What are your conditions of love? What must someone do to be loveable? What must you do to be loved? Many of you give and give and then are surprised that others do not give back in kind. Or you give and then you do not notice how much comes back to you from many sources because the sources you "want" or require may not be the ones responding.

Are you loved?

Answer this question instantly and immediately. Are you loved? Yes or No? Do not hesitate for that will tell you volumes about how you see the world. If you answered No, is that true? For if you say it is, then the one person who should always love you must not and that is the only person within your control – YOU! You should be able to count on one person to love you always and that is YOU!! Beyond that is just gravy as you say. If you cannot love YOU, then why should anyone else? Wouldn't they be foolish to love someone that does not deserve it? Do you want them to convince you that you are loveable or worth loving? What tells you that you are not loveable? If you love your Self and realize that you are made in the image of the Divine Creator, then that should be enough, but we know that it is not for so many of you.

Next, did you answer the question with a conditional "yes?" People may love you but not the ones you desire. Maybe you believe that your parent or parents do not love you. Is this really true? If it is, what have you done that makes you unlovable? If there is no answer that is viable, then is it a story you have about your life. Maybe that parent cannot love as you would like it to look. Most likely they do not love themselves so how can they love another? Maybe your conditional answer was about romantic love. Maybe you are alone in the world without a partner. Does that make you unlovable? Does it mean you are not worth loving or does it mean that right here, right now there is not another in your life. Again, we ask, "Do you love you?" Do you even like you?

Take time to redefine what you think love looks like and begin to look at all the conditions and rules you apply to love. Love is free and flows through the ethers toward each and every one of you. Stop and take a moment to get into the silence of the love that is vibrating about you and allow it into your world so that your universe of one can live in love.

We leave lovingly and long for peace.
Namaste

COMMIT

Anything is possible if you commit to it. That is a very simple statement and it is the complete and honest truth, but most of you are not willing to commit. You want to live your lives with one foot out the door so that you can always have an escape route. Commitment takes courage. It takes dedication. It takes time and it takes talent. The talent is in the act of committing.

What does commitment look like? It looks like staying the course even when it is difficult or scary or hard or emotionally or physically taxing. It means wanting something more than your freedom and your free will. Free will does not disappear with commitment, but it can feel that way sometimes because you cannot always take the easy way out once you have committed. There is commitment in relationship, there is commitment in a job, there is commitment to your Self and there is commitment to God.

What did you come here to do? This is a question so many of you ask on a regular basis. Let us say that you came here to heal. How do you go about this? Well, you could become a doctor of some sort, whether it be allopathic or holistic or naturopathic. You could be a nurse or a medical assistant. You could be a counselor or psychologist. You could be a Spiritual teacher or you could be a person who, through the laying on of hands, heals. Yes, that is possible. There are many modalities that allow for healing outside of the traditional roles. Maybe you simply are the world's best listener and for people as they tell their stories you help them heal by listening and reflecting back to them that which they seek. Now, no one or the other is better than the rest. It is not loftier to be a surgeon than it is to be a listener. Your society may say so, but it is not.

If you came here to heal, then you must find the method that is best for you and do the work. Once you find it, commit to the process of learning how to be the best healer you know how to be and do not judge the job. If you do not know why you are here, then begin to journey inside of your Self and learn what makes you light up, what makes you be in joy and what makes you feel complete. The answers are in there and the discovery of them will set you free. Commit to finding out.

We leave in a committed and loving way.
Namaste

FAITH

When life appears to be dealing you hands that are not winners or that seem impossible to play, that is the time to remember that faith is what carries you through. If your life is in chaos right now there is a reason. It is most likely a time of transition and change. It is the leaving of one way of being and the entering into another form of existence. The old ways no longer work and it is time for transformation and growth.

Why are these transitional times so scary or fraught with fear and trepidation? It is because it is truly a crossing over of a bridge in life that moves you further along your chosen path toward the enlightenment and life you desire. What lessons can you take with you? What have you learned from the upheaval? Transition is easy if you allow it to be, but most people in the human condition do not want the change to be simple or easy. It must have drama, it must have angst, and it must have heartache because without all of this your willingness to change is less. For some reason if it is not painful, it is not worth having. We question this position, but it is a choice many of you make.

The realization that something is no longer working or must change is not enough because you all become complacent in your way of living. It maybe not be fun or in your best and highest purpose, but it is a lot easier to remain stagnant than it is to change. Some of you may have been trying to change, but there was not enough impetus or urgency to force you to be more proactive in your search of the new path, so life intervenes with a bit more drama than is necessary. Drama for some reason gets your attention. Maybe you need to hear that you are not good enough at something or that you are not listening well enough to life. Rather than take offense at the fact you are not "perfect," listen to what is being said and take the parts that apply and change your life for the better so that the rest of what is coming can be more magnificent than what has just occurred.

Life is a series of opportunities that present themselves. It is your job to look life squarely in the eyes and choose that which is best for you. That which is best for you may not be what you have right now, but rather a much different path. Your guides and masters will often intervene to move you off the “safe” or familiar path into unknown realms of opportunity and growth.

We leave you in the excitement of life.
Namaste

DISBELIEF

Why do you focus on the impossibilities of life?

Why does it seem that you cannot
have what you "want?"

What do you "want?"

That is the real question --

"What do you want?"

Please sit for a few moments with this question. Allow it to rattle around your mind or psyche for a little while. If you can, sit with it in meditation and peace.

Most of you "want" things or something external. You want a relationship, a home, a car, a better job, more money or possessions that you believe will make you HAPPY or content or at peace. Nothing can be further from the truth. If you are not happy right here, right now without whatever you came up with on your list, then there is a hole in your Soul that needs filling. Attempting to fill those holes with things or possessions or people is futile because they are all transitory. You and your Soul connection with "what is" is what is missing.

Happiness and contentment can be found lying about anywhere you go if you are happy and content within because you are carrying it with you not without. It is the only luggage you need. When you read of the great mystics, they are often walking alone in the wilderness without food or water or companionship yet miracles occur for them that sustain them and lift them up to higher levels of consciousness. It is the burden of possessions that weighs you all down. It is the belief that possessions will complete you or make you seem okay. Why do people own mansions? Do they do it because they need to know that they live in a magnificent dwelling or do they do it so YOU know they live in a magnificent dwelling? Walk in to some magnificent homes. Is there love? Is there warmth? Is there joy? Things have no energy, love does. Caring does. Insight does.

Work on becoming alive. Stop waiting for life to happen and embrace where you are right here and right now and then begin the journey that says, "I am perfect as I am right now." If you do, your perfection will grow exponentially each and every day and magnificence will open where only sadness once dwelled.

We leave you ALIVE and in joy.
Namaste

BEAUTY

What is beauty?

Is it physical?

Is it nature?

Is it art?

Is it something that is universal?

What about the beauty of your being or your Soul if you will?

How do you touch beauty?

How do you access it?

There is a phrase that beauty is only skin deep, but that is not necessarily true, for true beauty emanates from within you out into the world. Your world has become obsessed with outward beauty and that, we are afraid is all too often skin deep. Worrying about how beautiful your skin or body appear is a way to keep from wondering or worrying about how beautiful your being is. What do you put out into the world? Is it peace, love, graciousness and kindness? Do you spend as much time on your inner grace and beauty as you do on the external? Do you spend as much money on the true Self as you do on the package that surrounds it? Do you worry that your Soul is not perfect or is it only your body – its shape, weight, clothes, hair and skin? An old Soul is something to cherish and explore, but are you more concerned about how old you look?

Life is about discovery and the journey of that discovery - Nothing more and nothing less. It is not about who can acquire more or overpower the weak or triumph over another. It is not about possessions other than the gift of possessing friends and people who seek you out for your wisdom and strength rather than your money and power. Please understand that there is nothing wrong with the acquisition of money or things, for that is a real lesson for some, but it is the use of that power, it is the manner of pursuit that matters most. Take the time to look at someone you have envied or thought you admired. What is their Soul? Who are they truly? Stop and take the time to assess what you have coveted and then take time to assess your own Soul and begin the journey to your own center to discover of what you are truly made.

That will be beautiful we guarantee.

We leave in grace and beauty.
Namaste

JOY

Are you joyful?
Every day?
Can you find joy in each day you are alive?

That is the goal or perhaps the lesson. In every moment and in every day and in every way there is joy. There is no reason that this cannot be true. You cannot provide to us the "evidence" that joy is not surrounding you at all times. Most of you are in the middle of the Emporium of Joy and you think the shelves are empty. Where are you looking? You are looking down and out and everywhere but inside of your Self to find the joy that is available to you right here, right now. What would it take for you to be joyful? The right answer is NOTHING. You choose it. You can choose it from the darkest place in your life because there does not have to be a reason. Choose laughter rather than tears or better yet, laugh until you cry. Why do you have to have a reason to be happy?

So many of you plod about life waiting for something good to happen. It is happening in every second of your life because you are alive and while you are alive you have choice and while you have choice you have joy – if you so choose.

How irritating are you finding this message right now? Our guess is plenty because you are all evidence building that this is not true. You are lining up all of your woes and trials and tribulations to "prove" that you have no reason to be happy or joyful or full of laughter. We are not wrong. You can laugh during a funeral if you so choose. Why would you? Because perhaps the person that is gone was wonderful fun and you can think of something that made you smile. Or perhaps the person that is gone was a difficult and unhappy person and without them you might find greater joy. You do not have to have a reason and there is no right and wrong. The point of this lesson is to let you know that YOU CHOOSE the emotions you have, they do not choose you. If you do not like that which you have, then change it, but do not seek outside of your Self for the change agent for it is not with-out, it is within. You can change today years of sadness and unhappiness by doing just that – choosing to not have it any longer.

We leave you in joy and love as always.

May your choices be for peace and joy.
Namaste

WORRY

What is worry?

Does it feel like low level anxiety to you?

Is it concern about the outcome of something important?

Is it concern about the outcome of just about everything?

Has worry ever changed any outcome?

There is a difference between thinking through a situation and worry. Worry is a non-productive emotion. It is similar to sitting in your car and just revving your engine over and over and over until your car overheats and you run out of gas. It gets you nowhere. Often it can dig you further into a situation for which you are seeking resolve. So how do you stop? Ah, that is the question.

One of the first steps is to consciously realize that you are worrying and to take a deep breath and sit back and begin to analyze the causes of the anxiety or worry. If you can get to the root of the problem you can begin to unwind the emotions and see the reason or reasons for the concerns. Let us say that something financial has occurred such as you have incurred a huge debt that you cannot pay. What are your options? Can you borrow the money without it being a huge burden? Can you work an extra job for a few months that would make the difference? Can you negotiate the amount to something less? Can you work out a payment plan that makes it possible to pay the debt and still live your life as you have? The best way around worry is to look at options, once you have those you can begin to buy your Self the breathing room you need to think clearly. Worry most often comes from fear and fear is a state of over thinking and seeing no options.

So, life and salvation is in the breath. As you begin to meditate you breathe so that you can begin to alter your state of consciousness and allow for your true Self to emerge and begin to communicate with you. As we have recommended many times, sit and breathe deeply. Breathe long cleansing breaths that truly fill your lungs with oxygen and allow your body, mind and Spirit to rest and be in tranquility and peace. Once you do this, the anxiety can begin to subside and with the cessation of it comes answers.

We leave you full of oxygen and in love.
Namaste

PATIENCE

Why are you impatient?

Do you believe that life is to happen on a certain timetable?

What is your agenda?

Why is it difficult to wait and allow life to unfold?

Most of you try to force life to happen. This is true even if you believe and feel as though you are drifting along with no seeming purpose or direction. Instead of enjoying this time of peaceful floating and creation you worry that you "should" be doing more or "should" be working harder or going to school or seeking the perfect job or finding the right mate or buying a home or living in a particular location. Why? If you truly desire something and you can feel that the desire is from an internal guidance, then pursue that avenue, but if you desire because of your head or belief system that says this will be best for you, stop and think for a bit. Life is as it should be in any moment and it can change from moment to moment in ways thought impossible if you simply sit and listen and act upon opportunity.

Let us say that you are currently going to school to improve your job or work potential. You are taking courses that may or may not relate to your actual work. Does this enliven you or upset you? Do you judge the classes individually and wonder, worry and obsess whether or not this will matter in the larger scheme of things? Perhaps a better approach would be to enjoy what you are learning and not worry about its later application, but rather dive into the learning process. The acquisition of knowledge is never a bad thing. It will come to you in surprising moments; perhaps years later, when you will think, "Ah that is why I learned that?" What pleasure do you derive from judging the classes and finding them not enough or judging your Self for the fact that you do not know in this moment the value of what you are doing?

Next let us say that you are looking for a different job and have not had any "luck" finding the job of your dreams. Are you aligned with your dreams? Do you truly know what you want and where you should be or are you trying to force the decision into some preconceived idea you have of what you should be doing. All things are but stepping stones on the way to something else. If you can realize that, you can be more content where you are right now rather than ruing your circumstances.

What if you long for a partner or mate? Do you bemoan being alone? Do you focus on what you don't have rather than what you do? Who would want to come into the chaos of your world at this point if you are spending your time listing all the things that you want to change and that are wrong or unpleasant? Think about the world you are creating and inviting others into and then maybe you will begin to see that it is you creating the void, not because you are not loveable or pretty or thin or rich or smart or whatever story you make up, but rather that you are chaotic and off balance. Even if someone wanted to come and play, how could they get in and survive the tumult?

So, as you go forth remember that peace and calm are the best places of creation. Take those five or ten or twenty minutes a day to sit and breathe and communicate with Self – True Self and you will begin to find the journey not one of waiting, but rather one of movement and love.

We leave in peace.
Namaste

OVERWHELM

Why do you feel overwhelmed?

What is it about your life *right now* that causes you to feel out of control, overworked, over committed and "under" capable?

Life is a series of lessons!

Fear is your biggest enemy.

Of what are you fearful?

Do you ask for what you want?

Do you ask for it in a way that enlivens and uplifts rather than demands and seeks?

Are you at peace with the flow of the universe and its gifts?

Do you trust that all will be as it should?

Do you listen?

Listen to your Self – Listen to your intuition and stop this crazy upset. You can always question your choices, but in most things your original choice is sufficient. It will be fine, whatever the choice. Life will move on and you will find joy. Allow for what has happened. The choice you made was for a reason, let it play out and get on to the next thing. Where are you next going? What do you next need to do? Where is the joy coming from next? Most of you live constrained by details and things to do to fill the time as life unfolds. Get on with the process of your life. Make a list of what needs be done next and just go get it done.

Life is a forceful river of energy and you are in for the ride, get into the flow of the water and into its strength and you will begin to feel energized and at peace once more. Keep your eyes up and ahead and the details will take care of themselves. Many opportunities are coming and you must be awake and aware.

We leave you with joy, understanding and most of all love.
Namaste

UNREST

Are you edgy and just off kilter?

Do you feel nervous and unsure?

Does life seem to be moving too quickly or too mysteriously for your tastes?

This is because you are not trusting the process of life. Life is not a simple, smooth path of only good and happy things. It is a journey which includes treacherous mountains, deep gorges, vast valleys and long wide plains. It is easy to get lost along the way of life because often we try to seek the path of least resistance or what seems the least resistance in the moment. Often times it is not the "least" but rather the "most" resistance that we are choosing. This comes from the desire to control the outcome. This is when you think that you know more than the forces of the universe or God.

Do you truly know what is "best" for you? Do you know what life experiences will most enrich and enliven you for your Soul's journey? We would tell you that you think you know, because most of you want it to be pretty pictures, filled with birds and flowers and sunshine and song. You want relationships that are loving and compatible and easy. You want work that is fulfilling and highly lucrative and rewarding or you want not to work at all. When you find your Selves in drudgery you choose to complain and moan rather than allow that for "right here, right now" this is what you are doing. The more you push against, the more you create chaos. This is not to say that you should accept ugly or difficult situations without thought. It means that you do not have to keep your Self enslaved by drudgery and sadness if you do not choose to do so.

The key to life is the realization that YOU CHOOSE. By this we mean you choose how to react, how to change, how to live with YOU in this moment. You do control YOU to the extent that you control the reaction to life. Do you see humour and possibility or do you see chaos and sadness and anger? What do you choose to feel and believe? Is the glass half empty or half full? Is life about possibility or about lack?

Sit with your Selves for a bit today and think about how you react to life. Are “they” doing it to you or are “You” doing it for you?

We leave as always in love.
Namaste

PATIENCE

It will come.

What does that statement feel like to you? Do you believe it? Do you question what "it" is? Just sit with the statement for a moment, "It will Come." Put the emphasis on each part differently.

IT will come.

It *WILL* come.

It will *COME*.

Each emphasis changes the meaning or impact slightly. Which one is best for you or closest to your desire?

Most of you sit and wait, some not so patiently, for IT to come your way. What is IT? What are you waiting for, longing for, wishing for, desiring? Do you even know or do you have a list so long that you cannot possibly fulfill it? We believe that most of you do not have a list or even truly know what IT is. Life is an adventure filled with events, people, places and occurrences. Some of them are wonderful and make your heart sing and others are scary and or upsetting or even fear creating. It is your attachment to them that causes the emotions to override the experience. Most things that are awful or scary only happen once or twice in life, yet you dwell on them and relive them in your minds over and over. Others of you may have experienced long periods of sadness, abuse, neglect or physical hardship, for this you have scars that are deep and raw, yet these too can be healed when you begin to walk away from that situation and into the life you were truly meant to live. One in which you love your Self enough to live fully in joy and light.

So what are you waiting for? Allow your Self the gift of sitting with this for a bit and truly thinking of what you desire. Patience is the best state of being because if you can think of what you want and then wait for life to bring it to you in some way, there is greater ease. If you desire or dream and then fuss and fret and despair over its not appearing, the wait will seem a lot longer and the reward less satisfying. So dream big today, enjoy the dream and then set it free to become reality. While you wait for the reality, get on with living and enjoying each moment that leads you down the path to your dreams.

We leave in great hope and love.
Namaste

ANXIETY

Do you feel the low rumble of nervousness and upset? Do you worry that things will not be as they should or more importantly as you "want?" This is the beginnings of anxiety. Anxiety is different than fear in that it is often caused by irrational beliefs or fears - ones that are not necessarily grounded in experience or reality. People experience many different types of anxiety. As mentioned, there is the low level rumble of something being off and there is the abject terror of an experience. Some are anxious about flying or driving on freeways or going into oceans or any body of water. Others worry about upcoming events or situations. It covers all bases and is often baseless, yet incredibly real.

Anxiety is the inability to quiet the mind and allow it to break down the fear or concern. What is causing the reaction? Now for most this cannot be known for it first begins rather unbidden and you just notice the touch of unease or unrest. There does not have to have been any event that triggers it, it just appears one day and stays. So we ask you to take a few moments to sit with your anxious state or your anxiety creating event. Breathe slowly and deeply as you sit and think about or look at the thing causing such upset. Imagine your Self in a quiet room with nothing but time to just sit calmly with this thing. The breath is the most important part of this as it calms the body and it is the body that is having the reaction. As you breathe and think of this anxiety causing event or thing notice where you are tense or stuck. Notice the thoughts going by and the feelings you have. When you hit a particularly big or difficult or scary thought, stop and sit with that thought. In essence, befriend it, give it attention and honor. This is a big thing for you on some level and it deserves care, compassion and recognition. You do not necessarily have to understand the reaction, just that it occurred when you were having this thought during this exercise. Sit with the thought as long as you can in compassion and relaxing breath and then when it feels comfortable, move on to other thoughts. If this is IT, then sit with it as long as you are able. Notice the changes in your breath, notice the feelings in your body, recognize the thoughts in your head and slowly breathe them all to a different state of more calm. We are not saying that you will be able to completely eradicate them with breath in one session, but notice how you are able to calm down, even if just a bit. It is the small steps toward calm that matter. This is the same with anxiety as it is with meditation. Small steps of breath and relaxation that will take you to a place of calm and ultimately bliss if you practice regularly and allow for miracles to occur.

We leave you calmly and in love.
Namaste

TRUST

Why do you not trust the process of life?

Why do you think of life in terms of good and bad decisions or good and bad events?

It is not so polarized. It is a series of events that move your life's journey forward. Nothing more and nothing less. The attachment to judgment is what keeps most of you small and unhappy. This is good or bad, right or wrong, happy or sad, fair or unfair. If you could learn the grace of just allowing for what happens to happen and not attaching a story or judgment to it, you would all be so much more at peace.

Let us say you are at work and something happens that you believe is not within integrity or within the parameters of fairness or correct behaviour. What do you do? Now we are not talking about illegal practices here, we are talking about interpretation of rules or boundaries or even some other person's behaviour. Do you become outraged? Do you become sad? Do you just move on? We would recommend that you notice the behaviour or action or policy and feel how you personally would handle the situation. Feel how good your decision would be and how at peace you would be if life were that way. Then rather than becoming outraged or whatever the emotion, take a few moments to sit with the situation and try to be at peace. If it is truly something that needs to be addressed with a superior, then do so, but wait for a few moments to understand your motivation. What makes you so right or righteous? Are you battling for the underdog? Exactly what is causing you to want to battle? Can the situation be handled in a calm and direct manner? Is there a way of solution that does not entail you becoming upset and angry and righteous? Again, we are not condoning behaviour that is harmful or ugly, but what we are saying is that you all need to stop and see where it truly affects you. If the integrity of the place in which you work is so far from your own, then perhaps it is time for you to seek other employ. It is the same with friends and even family.

What the Soul is seeking is balance and peace. It is not seeking right and wrong and up and down and in and out, it is seeking Peace and Balance. So many of you, for most of your lives, are trying to force a round peg into a square hole. You do not feel that you have a voice for your hurts and feelings and maybe you don't, but you can begin to have a voice if only you talk to your Self. Rather than judging and rating each event of life, you allow each event to occur and then you feel into your reaction to that event, life begins to move more peacefully. Most people are not "doing it to you," but rather are living their lives unconsciously and you are just in the wake of their unconsciousness. Actually what happens is the wake of their unconsciousness wakes you up and then you are bothered. Most of you spend your lives asleep in consciousness because to be truly cognizant of life around you, you must give up much of the story of living and simply live.

We leave you to contemplate Life and Living.
Namaste

LOVE

Why is there a scarcity of love?

This is a rather profound question, for in reality there is love abounding in the world and in the ethers of living. Love is all around you each and every moment but it is often not in the physical. Love is an energy. It is the transmuting of energetic support and calm. It is the knowing that all will be all right with the world and with life. It is knowing that you are never alone, for with love you have everything. Love does not have to come from another person to you or another thing to you. It is how you measure it, but this is not necessary or real. Love just is. That is it period. It just is. If you stand quietly in a room or space all alone and you allow (Ah, always the key word) your Self to just sit quietly and relax into the silence, you will feel love.

Love is the quiet that brings you calm. Love is the sweetness of knowing all is right. Love is the strength you derive from day-to-day living. Love is all there is. It is just like the Beatles' song said, "All you need is love....Love is all you need."

So why do most of you spend your lives seeking it outside of your Selves? What is it about another person showing you love that has more meaning than you showing it to your Self? Many of you derive love from "safe" sources, from small children or from pets. This is fine, but why can you not trust that if you were to love your Self fully and completely, without outside validation that this would be okay or suitable or sufficient? Most of you use the fact that you do not have someone or enough people outside of you loving you, so therefore you are not loveable. This is simply not true and yet many of you predicate your lives on believing or judging your Self to be "unlovable" or worse yet, not worthy of love.

Everyone is worthy of love even the most heinous person deserves love because perhaps if they could feel the love they would not be so heinous.

Love is the energy that transmutes hatred. Love is the energy that brings lightness to the dark. Love is the healing process of allowing each Soul to reach out to another and give light. During this time of meditation and study of this message, take a few moments to extend love to the most important person in your world – You.

We leave you in much love and hope for your future feelings of being loved.
Namaste

PEACE

So many of you are not at peace. You do not find peace in your daily living; you do not find peace in your work, families, cars, or world. You long for world peace and yet you cannot find it in your own backyard. So many of you rail against the leaders of the world and demand that they find peace and solutions to the vast differences that are affecting your globe at this time, but yet you cannot smile and allow another car in front of you or a person in line. Love, peace and harmony begin with you. No, you may not be able to stop the wars that are everywhere in your world, but you can stop the personal wars and that is the first step.

Self-hatred or loathing does not serve you and it does not serve the planet. So you are lazy or fat or ugly or stupid or whatever you choose to use as a label for your Self – this only allows you to keep your Self small. That is all it serves to do. It does not make you a better person, It does not make you a more humble or honest person. It does not make you a more willing child of God to be constantly at your Self with complaints and fault finding. What serves God and this world you live in, is for you to find within your Self the strength, the courage, the honesty to be who you truly are – a child of God.

Each of you is born with gifts and then it is your job or quest, if you will, to be able to find the ways in which to share those gifts with the world. Most of you want to handicap your Self so that your gifts become secondary to your purpose for being. You are not alone in this, but you alone can stop it. As you enter into a new way of living, stop the madness of fault finding and begin the excavation of your true Self. Uplift and support YOU as you are. Yes, you have faults and challenges and other things that may make it difficult or harder to share your gifts, but if each day you offer at least one gift to the world, it will slowly begin to transform.

Please try to go forth in the world today and find the joy that is called living and find the peace that is called love – love of Self first and then your fellow man.

We leave in hope for all of you.
Namaste

PERSISTENCE

How willing are you to persist?

How long will you attempt something before you give up or rethink your motivation?

You live in an instant society where immediate gratification is the norm not the exception. It is a society of accumulation of things and wealth, but one that all too often overlooks the greater rewards of Spirit.

What is your Soul worth? Please do not just read this and then move on. Stop and think about what your Soul and its needs are worth to you? You run about in your lives and are so busy earning, learning, buying, visiting and doing that you rarely take time to stop and just be. Can you just be in the moment without thoughts of what is to come or what just happened or where you need to be next? Are you present with your Self and others? What matters?

In the end there is only You. There are no things, no possessions, no trappings of wealth or affluence. Just You and your Self. What will you have to present at the end? What will you show for your journey here on earth? Many of you long for fame or recognition. You live in society that says your 15 minutes of fame are more important than any thing else. You worship the celebrity or the billionaire. Some of you may adore or follow a Spiritual leader, but do you do so because of their message of because it is cool to be a groupie of a famous leader? What is your motivation, we ask again?

If you follow the Dalai Lama is it because you understand and embrace his teachings? Do you incorporate his religion of kindness into your life or do you just quote what he says and relate experiences? It is the same with Sai Baba or Mother Theresa or the Pope or Billy Graham. Do you take the time to allow the message or the lessons or the example to infiltrate your life and come to rest and implant on your Soul? Again, we would ask if you really need any of them or can you just take the time to have your own personal relationship with God, The Almighty or whatever you call the omnipotent force of the Universe. Do not get caught up in semantics when it comes to this energy. Do not give your opinion or lectures about how you don't believe or like certain words because that is how you stay small and out of the game.

Get into the game of living which is to discover, nurture and uplift your Spirit so that you may truly understand the magnificence of what life has to offer. It is not a TV or telephone or a car or a house or any of those things. Those are all ancillary to life. Be careful what you worship. If you put your eyes upon that which matters, the rest will fall into place and then your life will truly begin to work.

We leave in the hope that you can begin the true journey to Self.
Namaste

PITY

Do you want pity?
Do you feel that you deserve to be pitied?

Do you pity others?

What is pity?

It is a form of victimhood that keeps you and others small. People seek pity because they do not stand fully in their own light and request that which they need and deserve. Pity is a cop out from accepting responsibility for your actions or situation.

Often people will make themselves into carpets upon which others tread and then when this happens they become resentful. Most of you put your Selves where you are and then you wish you were not there. So get out. Take responsibility for your life, actions and the consequences thereof. It is very easy to want to abdicate your participation in matters that are not pleasant or easy. If you are in debt, is it of your own doing? Then stop whining about it and get out of debt. You may have to do without “things” that are really not necessary or change for awhile the way in which you use money, but ultimately you will be debt free. If you are overweight, stop the behaviour that is causing it. Change how you eat. Change how you move and exercise your body or simply change your relationship with food.

So much of life is changing your relationship with the problem. First, if you think it is a problem, it is – so start there. Next focus on what you want, not on what you don’t want or don’t have. You are calling into being that which you focus upon. We have shared all this before, but it is time for you to rise up and take command of life rather than be at the effect of the consequences. Wake up and march into life boldly and deal with the details as they occur rather than waiting until the details become so large that they seem insurmountable. This too is a perception, but it is easier to start when things are small and eradicate them rather than having to eat the elephant one bite at a time. We mix our metaphors, but what we are saying is that the time is now to take a hold of life and control the ways in which you create your own chaos.

We leave with love.
Namaste

ORDER FORM

Yes!

would love to order copies of this book for my friends and family so they too can begin the discovery of Self!!!

For ordering information you may do one or any of the following:

Email Heather Cronrath at Headcoach1@aol.com

Visit Heather Cronrath at her website:
www.headcoachenterprises.com

Write Heather Cronrath
PO Box 124
Scottsdale, AZ 85252

Thank you for your interest and support!!!